Carefree Cookbook

A collection of recipes for the mother with small children, covering every occasion she may have to cook for, from feeding the children every day and at their parties, to entertaining friends for dinner or a buffet party for twelve or twenty-four.

Christine Cooper
and
Angela Hildesley

For Mark, Paul, Lucy and William who made this book necessary, and for our friends who allowed us to pinch their best recipes, and thereby made it possible.

Hamlyn

London · New York · Sydney · Toronto

Contents

Acknowledgements

The authors and publishers thank the following for their co-operation in supplying photographs for the book:

Bordeaux Direct: page 63
Farmhouse English Cheese (Milk Marketing Board): page 19
H. J. Heinz Company Limited: page 27
Kellogg Company of Great Britain Limited: page 51
The Pastry Bureau: page 59
Spring's Ma Made: page 31
John West Foods Limited: page 23
White Fish Authority: page 55

Published by
The Hamlyn Publishing Group Limited
London · New York · Sydney · Toronto
Astronaut House, Feltham, Middlesex, England
© Copyright The Hamlyn Publishing Group
Limited 1975
ISBN 0 600 31879 6
Printed in England by Chapel River Press
Andover, Hampshire
Photography by John Lee
Line drawings by Hayward Art Group

Introduction

This book is written for mothers with small children by mothers with small children. It has largely been written when the children were asleep, in the hope of making life easier when they are very much awake.

Neither of us is a professional cook and so our methods are taken more from experience than from books. We are used to being distracted when cooking and have assembled recipes where urgent summonses to referee yet another rumpus or cries for help don't cause catastrophes. People who cook for pleasure are served to saturation by cookbooks, magazines and newspapers; people who cook for survival, we feel, deserve a simpler, more direct and sympathetic guide which helps them to provide interesting and nourishing food without stretching either their pockets or their patience. In our experience cooking time has best been staggered through the day. Anyone who has prepared a meal and themselves for guests, whilst simultaneously bathing a couple of high-spirited children, will know that from five to eight in the evening is no time for concentrated cooking. Because of this we have devoted one section of the book to children's lunches which can be adapted as evening meals, as well as including seven complete menus for entertaining which can all be prepared well in advance.

We feel it important that food be freshly cooked for the children, but since small children usually eat rather dull food, and that in small quantities, there is a great temptation just to offer them last night's leftovers and be done with it. Unfortunately, their dislike of second-hand stuffed peppers is only equalled by their father's dislike of reheated baked beans, so we have emphasized the importance of planning meals as a continuous campaign rather than as individual skirmishes.

We have avoided too many technical terms and are not in the least dogmatic about either equipment or even, in some cases, ingredients. Many great scientific discoveries have been accidents, but few of them have been as successful as the accidents that happen to meals in thousands of homes every day. You probably have enough equipment already to cope with most of our recipes. However, there are a few things which we feel make the cook's life easier. A couple of really good knives are most important; these need not be expensive, but they must be kept sharp. A good pair of kitchen scissors is excellent for cutting up bacon and trimming meat. A large chopping board, a non-stick milk saucepan for sauces, a couple of large casseroles which can be used on top of the stove, in the oven and put straight on to the table and a good selection of baking tins and pie dishes (these can often be found at jumble sales for next to nothing) are all invaluable. Finally, we feel that cooking without a blender and a mixer is like Do-It-Yourself without a power drill! These are not luxuries but essentials, and it is worth economising on food for a few weeks to save up and buy them. Each can now be bought for about £10, and they open up a whole new range of recipes.

At the end of the book, on the endpapers, are useful facts and figures and some suggested standbys for your store cupboard. We have covered every situation you are likely to have to contend with in the kitchen, from feeding the children to a buffet party for twenty-four. Although this is not a comprehensive collection of recipes, it is our choice of food to help you through the day, and we hope you will enjoy using this book.

Angela Hitchsley

Christine Cooper

Freezing notes

One of the best friends of a family with small children is a home freezer. Although it may not save you enormous sums of money it does undoubtedly save time. However, if you shop at a specialised freezer shop some things are much cheaper, and most of them are the sort of things that children eat in large quantities, such as sausages and fish fingers. If you come in at lunchtime exhausted from a long fight in the shops, it is marvellous to feel that you can produce a meal in five minutes flat. Although many magazines and articles on the subject of freezing stress that you must get the biggest and best, if this is beyond you and for that matter your purse, there are other ways. One of the best, and cheapest, is to buy a second-hand ice cream conservator. These can be bought for less than £20, though you must only use them for food which has already been frozen. They work very well, and are a very good start until you can afford a proper freezer. Time, as we have said, is the biggest asset. It doesn't take much longer to make two shepherd's pies than one; you eat one and freeze the other, saving yourself half an hour next week. If you are in the mood, and have a fairly peaceful day, you can cook like mad and fill up the freezer with mince, stews, pies, uncooked pastry and vegetables, so that if you are tired, or just don't feel like cooking (and we all get days like that) you can open the freezer and take out a complete meal.

A good freezer shop is worth finding, and do shop around, as often there is more than one of these per town, and the prices vary considerably. These shops are open to everyone; even if you haven't a freezer you can still take advantage of the cheaper frozen food. They will usually split large boxes up, so you needn't eat fish fingers all the week.

Almost everything can be frozen in strong polythene bags with a simple twist to close them. If your freezer is small it is worth freezing food in square polythene boxes first, and turning the blocks out into bags. These blocks are then very easy to stack on top of one another, and you don't lose valuable space.

Cakes which are iced are best frozen on a plate first, and then put into bags. The rolls of polythene bags are the most convenient to buy, and plastic ties usually come with them. It is worth labelling the food, as although you yourself may know which is curry sauce as opposed to stewed apple, frozen blocks do look very much alike and your unsuspecting husband, left on his own for a day, may get a nasty surprise. You can buy very cheap bundles of tie-on labels, and if you want the stick-on variety cut up some luggage labels – much cheaper and just as effective as the special freezer labels they will try and sell you. When writing use a lead pencil or a good ballpoint pen, as anything else may disappear in a month or two and you'll be back to square one. We both have freezers, and the second-hand one has paid for itself in under a year – and that is only in the monetary sense. In time and temper saved, it paid for itself long before the year was up! Here is a list of food which we have found to be most useful kept in the freezer:

fresh breadcrumbs
chopped parsley and chives
uncooked crumble topping
uncooked pastry in 8-oz. (225-g.) packs
bread rolls
apple purée, for puddings and apple sauce
flans
pies
stews
basic mince
fish cakes

Family food

This section is a collection of simple, everyday main meals. Most of them are pretty basic, but we have chosen them because they are suitable for all ages, economical and easy to prepare. We have not split this section into lunches and suppers, as which of these is your main meal of the day obviously depends on whether or not your husband and your children come home at lunchtime.

In order to make things easier, and to save time, we have arranged everything in sections according to the main ingredient – e.g., beef, lamb, pork, etc. Puddings are kept in a separate section, as not everybody wants one every day.

All the quantities given are enough for an average family with two or three small children.

Soups

Mixed vegetable soup

With bread and cheese, this is a complete meal.

Imperial/Metric	American
1 large onion	1 large onion
2 leeks	2 leeks
3 large carrots	3 large carrots
3 potatoes	3 potatoes
2 stalks celery	2 stalks celery
any other vegetables you care to add	any other vegetables you care to add
little butter for frying	little butter for frying
1½ pints/scant litre chicken stock	4 cups chicken stock
1 tablespoon chopped parsley (optional)	1 tablespoon chopped parsley (optional)

Chop all the vegetables coarsely first. Melt a little butter in a large saucepan and fry the onion and the leeks first, for 5 minutes. Add the remaining vegetables and fry for a further 5 minutes, stirring from time to time, to prevent them catching on the bottom. Add the stock, and bring to the boil. Simmer for 15 minutes or until the vegetables are tender. The carrots will take the longest, so try them. Add the chopped parsley if you have some. Check the seasoning, but go carefully, as the stock may have enough in it already.

You can either eat this soup just as it is, with the chunks of vegetables, or if you like purée it.

Cooking time about 30 minutes

Illustrated on page 19

Sweetcorn chowder

Imperial/Metric	American
4 oz./100 g. streaky bacon	5 slices bacon
1 large onion, chopped	1 large onion, chopped
1 stalk celery, chopped	1 stalk celery, chopped
1 green pepper, blanched and chopped	1 green sweet pepper, blanched and chopped
2 potatoes, diced	2 potatoes, diced
bay leaf	bay leaf
¾ pint/4 dl. water	2 cups water
salt and pepper	salt and pepper
1 oz./25 g. flour	¼ cup flour
½–¾ pint/3–4 dl. milk	1½–2 cups milk
1 can sweetcorn	1 can corn
chopped parsley	chopped parsley

Cut the bacon into pieces with scissors and fry gently until beginning to brown, then add the onion and celery and fry gently for 5 minutes. Add the green pepper, potatoes, bay leaf and water and bring to the boil. Add salt and pepper to taste and simmer until the potatoes are just tender, then draw aside. Blend the flour with a little of the milk until smooth, add to the soup and stir until boiling. Add the rest of the milk along with the sweetcorn and stir until boiling again. Sprinkle with chopped parsley and serve with hot toast and butter.

Cooking time about 35 minutes

Ham and pea soup with frankfurters

Imperial/Metric	American
1 lb./450 g. dried peas	2 cups dried peas
1 ham bone or knuckle	1 ham bone
4 pints/2¼ litres water	2½ quarts water
1 onion	1 onion
salt and pepper	salt and pepper
milk	milk
8 oz./225 g. frankfurters	½ lb. frankfurters
knob of butter	knob of butter

Wash the peas and leave to soak overnight in plenty of cold water. Soak the ham bone if necessary; if a ham bone isn't available use the water left from boiling a ham. Drain the peas and put in a large saucepan with the water, ham bone and onion. Cover and cook until the peas are soft. Remove the bone and liquidise or sieve the soup. Taste; adjust seasoning and add milk if the soup is too strong. Slice the frankfurters and add to the soup with the butter; simmer for 10 minutes. Serve with rye or black bread.
Cooking time 1½ hours

Leek and potato soup

Imperial/Metric	American
2 oz./50 g. butter	¼ cup butter
1 onion	1 onion
3 large leeks	3 large leeks
6 medium-sized potatoes	6 medium-sized potatoes
1½ pints/scant litre chicken stock	4 cups chicken stock
¼ pint/1½ dl. single cream or top of the milk	⅔ cup coffee cream or half and half
1 tablespoon chopped parsley	1 tablespoon chopped parsley
salt and pepper	salt and pepper

Melt the butter in a large saucepan and fry the onion and leeks, chopped coarsely, for 5 minutes with the lid on. Add the diced potatoes and fry a further 2 minutes, stirring from time to time. Add the stock and bring to the boil. Simmer for about 20 minutes until the potatoes are soft. Put into the blender and liquidise until smooth. Return to the pan and add the cream and parsley just before serving. Season to taste at the end, as the stock may be salty.
Cooking time about 30 minutes

French onion soup

Very quick and simple to make.

Imperial/Metric	American
3 large onions	3 large onions
knob of butter	knob of butter
1 teaspoon sugar	1 teaspoon sugar
2 pints/generous litre water	5 cups water
2 beef stock cubes	2 beef bouillon cubes
salt and pepper	salt and pepper
4 slices toast	4 slices toast
4 oz./100 g. Cheddar cheese, grated	1 cup grated Cheddar cheese
little white wine (optional)	little white wine (optional)

Slice the onions thickly, melt the butter in a heavy saucepan and fry the onions until golden, not burnt, then sprinkle on the sugar. Add the water and stock cubes and bring to the boil. Simmer for half an hour. Season. Pour the soup into individual earthenware bowls (Pyrex also will do), put one slice of toast in each dish, cover with the grated cheese and put the dishes under a hot grill until the cheese becomes crisp and golden. A little white wine added to the stock greatly improves this soup, but it is not vital.
Cooking time about 40 minutes

Cream of cauliflower and watercress soup

This is a delicious and rather unusual soup.

Imperial/Metric	American
2 medium-sized onions	2 medium-sized onions
2 oz./50 g. butter	¼ cup butter
2 oz./50 g. flour	½ cup flour
2 pints/generous litre water or water and milk	5 cups water or water and milk
salt and white pepper	salt and white pepper
1 medium-sized cauliflower	1 medium-sized cauliflower
1 bunch watercress	1 bunch watercress
¼ pint/1½ dl. double cream	⅔ cup whipping cream
knob of butter	knob of butter

Peel and slice the onions, melt the butter (it is worth using butter for this soup) in a heavy saucepan, add the onions and cook gently until soft. Stir in the flour and cook for 1 minute, then slowly add the liquid (try 1 pint each of milk and water for a richer soup). Add salt and pepper and simmer. Wash the

cauliflower and break into small pieces, discarding leaves that are large and tough and reserving the small leaves. Drop the cauliflower, not leaves, into a pan of boiling salted water and boil for 2 minutes; drain and add to the onion mixture; simmer for 15 minutes. Wash the watercress and discard any wilted leaves and tough stems, then chop roughly and add to the soup with the small cauliflower leaves. Simmer for 10 minutes, cool slightly, then purée the soup. Reheat just before serving to preserve the watercress green, add the cream and a knob of butter and taste for seasoning.
Cooking time about 40 minutes

Garlic bread

Imperial/Metric	American
1 French loaf	**1 French loaf**
2 cloves garlic, crushed	**2 cloves garlic, crushed**
4 oz./100 g. butter	**½ cup butter**
salt and pepper	**salt and pepper**

Cut the loaf into 1-inch (2½-cm.) slices, not quite all the way through, so that it's still in one piece. Add the garlic to the butter and beat until soft and well mixed. Season well. Spread over each side of the slices, keeping a little for the top. Wrap the whole loaf in foil and seal the edges well. Put into a moderate oven for about 30 minutes or more. It should be crisp outside and hot and soft inside.
Cooking time about 30 minutes
Oven temperature 350°F., 180°C., Gas Mark 4

Variation
Cheese bread Substitute 4 oz. (100 g., 1 cup) grated Cheddar for the garlic and make in the same way.

Fish
Haddock or cod baked with bacon

Imperial/Metric	American
1 small onion	**1 small onion**
2 tablespoons oil	**3 tablespoons oil**
1 small can tomatoes	**1 small can tomatoes**
salt and pepper	**salt and pepper**
1 lb./450 g. haddock or cod fillets	**1 lb. haddock or cod fillets**
8 thin rashers streaky bacon	**8 thin slices bacon**
chopped parsley	**chopped parsley**
4 oz./100 g. mushrooms (optional)	**1 cup mushrooms (optional)**

Finely chop the onion and fry in the oil until soft; add the can of tomatoes and cook for a few minutes. Put this mixture in a shallow ovenproof dish, season, and place the fish on top of it. Remove the rinds from the bacon and put it over the fish. Cover and cook in a moderate oven for 30 minutes; remove the cover for the last 10 minutes to crisp the bacon. Sprinkle with parsley. The addition of the mushrooms, lightly fried, to the tomato mixture is very good.
Cooking time 30 minutes
Oven temperature 350°F., 180°C., Gas Mark 4

Fish crumble

This is very like fish pie, but is much more filling, and has a very good crunchy top.

Imperial/Metric	American
filling	filling
2 oz./50 g. margarine	**¼ cup margarine**
1 large onion, chopped	**1 large onion, chopped**
2 oz./50 g. flour	**½ cup flour**
¾ pint/4 dl. milk	**2 cups milk**
2 hard-boiled eggs, chopped	**2 hard-cooked eggs, chopped**
1 small can sweetcorn	**1 small can corn**
1 small packet frozen peas	**1 small package frozen peas**
1 lb./450 g. cod, cooked and flaked	**1 lb. cod, cooked and flaked**
topping	topping
2 oz./50 g. margarine	**¼ cup margarine**
4 oz./100 g. plain flour	**1 cup all-purpose flour**
2 oz./50 g. cheese, grated	**½ cup grated cheese**

To make the filling, melt the margarine in a saucepan, add the onion and fry for 10 minutes. Add the flour and cook for a further 2 minutes. Blend in the milk to make a sauce and stir till thickened. Remove from the heat and add the chopped eggs, sweetcorn, peas and fish. Season and put into a casserole.

To make the topping, rub the margarine into the flour until it is like breadcrumbs. Add the grated cheese, mix well and sprinkle over the fish mixture. Cook in a moderately hot oven for 30–40 minutes till golden.
Cooking time 30–40 minutes
Oven temperature 375°F., 190°C., Gas Mark 5

Kedgeree

There are no special rules for this dish; add more or less fish or rice.

Imperial/Metric	American
12 oz./350 g. smoked haddock or white fish	¾ lb. smoked haddock or white fish
8 oz./225 g. rice	1 cup rice
1 medium-sized onion	1 medium-sized onion
butter	butter
1 teaspoon curry powder (optional)	1 teaspoon curry powder (optional)
2 hard-boiled eggs	2 hard-cooked eggs
2 tablespoons sultanas (optional)	3 tablespoons white raisins (optional)
1 egg	1 egg
salt and pepper	salt and pepper
top of the milk	half and half
watercress	watercress

Place the fish in a large frying pan or a baking dish, cover with water, cover the dish and simmer or poach in a moderate oven for 15 minutes. Drain the fish, remove skin and bones and flake. Boil the rice according to the type, rinse and leave to drain. Thinly slice the onion and fry in butter, do not use margarine just this once. When the onion is golden add the curry powder, fry for 1 minute, then add the fish, chopped hard-boiled eggs, sultanas and rice. Stir all this thoroughly with a fork. Lightly beat the egg and stir into the kedgeree with a knob of butter and seasoning. Stir in a little top of the milk if it is too dry. Turn on to a heated dish and garnish with watercress.

Cooking time about 25 minutes
Oven temperature 350°F., 180°C., Gas Mark 4

Mackerel in foil with mustard sauce

Imperial/Metric	American
4 large mackerel, cleaned, with the heads removed	4 large mackerel, cleaned, with the heads removed
salt and pepper	salt and pepper
few porridge oats	little oatmeal
mustard sauce	mustard sauce
3 tablespoons mayonnaise	¼ cup mayonnaise
1 teaspoon made English mustard	1 teaspoon made English mustard

Season the insides of the fish with salt and pepper and press a few porridge oats over the outsides. This helps absorb some of the oil from the fish, as they are rather rich. Place each in a piece of foil and completely enclose each fish. Place in a baking dish and cook in a moderate oven for 30 minutes.

Meanwhile mix the mayonnaise and the mustard together and put in a dish. Unwrap the fish and serve with plain boiled potatoes sprinkled with parsley, a tomato salad and the mustard mayonnaise.

Cooking time 30 minutes
Oven temperature 325°F., 160°C., Gas Mark 3

Portuguese plaice

Imperial/Metric	American
6 canned sardines	6 canned sardines
6 tablespoons fresh white breadcrumbs	½ cup fresh white bread crumbs
rind and juice of 1 lemon	rind and juice of 1 lemon
½ onion, chopped	½ onion, chopped
1 egg	1 egg
salt and pepper	salt and pepper
2 teaspoons chopped parsley	2 teaspoons chopped parsley
6 small plaice fillets	6 small flounder fillets
1 oz./25 g. butter	2 tablespoons butter
sauce (optional)	sauce (optional)
milk	milk
½ oz./15 g. butter	1 tablespoon butter
½ oz./15 g. flour	2 tablespoons flour
salt and pepper	salt and pepper
chopped parsley	chopped parsley

Mash the sardines and combine with the breadcrumbs in a bowl. Put the lemon rind, onion, egg, salt and pepper in the blender and blend until smooth. Add to the sardine mixture with the parsley and mix together well. Spread the mixture over the plaice fillets and roll up. Arrange in a buttered ovenproof dish, pour over the lemon juice and dot with butter. Cover with a lid or some foil and bake in a moderate oven for 20–30 minutes. If you like a sauce, strain off the liquor in the baking dish and make up to 8 fluid oz. (2 dl., 1 cup) with milk. Melt the butter in a pan, stir in the flour, add the milk and bring to the boil, stirring. Season to taste and add the parsley. Cook for a few minutes, then pour over the plaice.

Cooking time 20–30 minutes
Oven temperature 350°F., 180°C., Gas Mark 4
Illustrated on page 23

Salmon pie

This is delicious, rather like a soufflé, but foolproof.

Imperial/Metric	American
1 lb./450 g. mashed potatoes	2 cups mashed potatoes
milk and butter	milk and butter
1 egg, separated	1 egg, separated
1 8-oz./227-g. can salmon, flaked	1 8-oz. can salmon, flaked
½ teaspoon grated lemon rind	½ teaspoon grated lemon rind
3 oz./75 g. cheese, grated	¾ cup grated cheese
½ teaspoon mustard	½ teaspoon mustard
salt and pepper	salt and pepper

Make the mashed potatoes really creamy with plenty of milk and butter. Add the egg yolk and beat well. Add the flaked fish, lemon rind and 2 oz. (50 g., ½ cup) grated cheese, beat well, and season with mustard, salt and pepper. Put into a buttered ovenproof dish which is not too wide across the top. Beat the egg white, fold the remaining cheese into it, and spread over the fish mixture. Put into a hot oven for 15–20 minutes, till the top is golden.

Cooking time 15–20 minutes
Oven temperature 425°F., 220°C., Gas Mark 7
Illustrated on page 23

Salmon pasties

Very good for picnics.

Imperial/Metric	American
pastry	pastry
8 oz./225 g. plain flour	2 cups all-purpose flour
½ teaspoon salt	½ teaspoon salt
4 oz./100 g. margarine or lard	½ cup margarine or lard
4 oz./100 g. Cheddar cheese, grated	1 cup grated Cheddar cheese
water to mix	water to mix
little milk to glaze	little milk to glaze
filling	filling
2 medium-sized potatoes	2 medium-sized potatoes
1 7-oz./198-g. can salmon	1 7-oz. can salmon
2 hard-boiled eggs	2 hard-cooked eggs
4 oz./100 g. frozen peas	¾ cup frozen peas
salt and pepper	salt and pepper

Make the pastry in the usual way, adding the cheese after rubbing in the fat. To make the filling, peel the potatoes and cut into small dice. Drain the salmon, reserving the liquid; remove the skin and bone and flake the fish. Chop the eggs and mix with the salmon. Add the potatoes, peas and salmon liquid and season. Roll out the pastry and cut into six circles: use a saucer and cut round it. Divide the salmon mixture into six and place in the centres of the pastry circles. Brush the edges of the pastry with cold water, seal the edges together and knock up the edges with the back of a knife. Brush with a little milk. Place on a greased baking sheet and cook in a moderately hot oven for 40 minutes. Serve hot, or cold for picnics.

Cooking time 40 minutes
Oven temperature 400°F., 200°C., Gas Mark 6

Cold fish mould

Imperial/Metric	American
1 lb./450 g. white fish, cod or coley	1 lb. white fish, cod or haddock
milk and water	milk and water
½ pint/3 dl. thick white sauce	1¼ cups thick white sauce
1 hard-boiled egg, chopped	1 hard-cooked egg, chopped
3 tablespoons mayonnaise	¼ cup mayonnaise
1 tablespoon lemon juice	1 tablespoon lemon juice
1 tablespoon chopped parsley	1 tablespoon chopped parsley
1 tablespoon chopped gherkins and capers	1 tablespoon chopped dill pickles and capers
salt and pepper	salt and pepper

Poach the fish for 10 minutes in a mixture of milk and water just to cover it. Flake the fish. Make a white sauce with the fish liquor in the usual way, but add a little extra flour at the beginning to ensure it is thick enough. Fold all the ingredients into the sauce and season well. Pour into a previously wetted pudding basin and allow to go cold. When really cold turn out and decorate with parsley.

This is really a cold fish pie and is very good in the summer with salad. Add some shrimps or prawns if you have them to decorate or some tomatoes cut in quarters and some sprigs of parsley, otherwise it looks rather pale.

Cooking time about 10 minutes

Beef

Beef is always expensive, but it is worthwhile buying the best quality you can afford, so that you are not paying for too much fat and gristle.

Cauliflower moussaka

Imperial/Metric	American
2 medium-sized onions	2 medium-sized onions
1 lb./450 g. minced beef	1 lb. ground beef
little oil	little oil
1 small cauliflower	1 small cauliflower
1 teaspoon cinnamon	1 teaspoon cinnamon
1 teaspoon mixed herbs	1 teaspoon mixed herbs
1 tablespoon chopped parsley	1 tablespoon chopped parsley
salt and pepper	salt and pepper
1 15-oz./425-g. can tomatoes	1 15-oz. can tomatoes
1 lb./450 g. potatoes	1 lb. potatoes
topping	topping
1 oz./25 g. margarine	2 tablespoons margarine
1 oz./25 g. flour	¼ cup flour
½ pint/3 dl. milk	1¼ cups milk
2 oz./50 g. cheese, grated	½ cup grated cheese
1 egg	1 egg

Grease a deep, fairly large casserole. Peel and chop the onions. Fry the meat with a little oil if necessary, add the onions and cook for a few minutes. Break the cauliflower into small pieces, wash and cook for 3 minutes in a pan of salted boiling water, drain well. Add the cinnamon, herbs and parsley to the meat and season well. Drain and slice the tomatoes, reserving the liquor. Peel and thinly slice the potatoes. Put one layer of potatoes in the casserole, cover with half the meat, the cauliflower, the tomatoes, then the rest of the meat and finally the remaining potatoes. Pour over the tomato liquor.

To make the topping, melt the margarine, add the flour, slowly add the milk and bring to the boil, stirring constantly. Simmer for a few minutes, then add the cheese and remove from the heat. Add the lightly beaten egg and season. Pour over the casserole and cook covered in a moderately hot oven for 1 hour, then remove the lid and cook uncovered for 20 minutes. Serve with some warmed bread and a green salad. This dish improves with reheating.
Cooking time 1 hour 20 minutes
Oven temperature 375°F., 190°C., Gas Mark 5

Basic stew and variations

Imperial/Metric	American
1 lb./450 g. stewing meat	1 lb. stewing meat
2 tablespoons flour	3 tablespoons flour
1 large onion	1 large onion
2 carrots	2 carrots
2 tablespoons oil or 2 oz./50 g. dripping	2 tablespoons oil or ¼ cup meat drippings
¾ pint/4 dl. beef stock made with 1 stock cube and water	2 cups beef stock made with 1 bouillon cube and water
bay leaf	bay leaf
salt and pepper	salt and pepper
dumplings (optional)	dumplings (optional)
3 oz./75 g. suet	⅔ cup shredded suet
8 oz./225 g. self-raising flour	2 cups all-purpose flour sifted with 2 teaspoons baking powder
salt and pepper	salt and pepper
water to mix	water to mix

Cut the meat into uniform pieces removing as much fat as possible. Put the flour into a polythene bag and shake the meat in it so that the meat is well coated. Prepare and slice the vegetables. Fry the onion in the heated oil or dripping until transparent, remove from the pan to a casserole, fry the meat for a few minutes then add the remaining flour. Stir in the stock and seasonings, bring to the boil, then pour into the casserole and add the carrots. Cook, covered, in a moderate oven for 2½ hours.

Mix the dumpling ingredients together, then add enough water to make a soft dough. Shape into balls and drop them on to the top of the stew half an hour before the end of the cooking time.
Cooking time 2½ hours
Oven temperature 325°F., 160°C., Gas Mark 3

Variations
This is the simplest stew there is; to make it more interesting add some, or any, of the following:
A few bacon rinds, or a couple of rashers of streaky bacon when you fry the onion.
Some beer, cider or wine instead of all stock.
A little green pepper with the onion.
A turnip, parsnip, or a couple of stalks of celery with the carrot.
Fifteen minutes before the end of cooking time add baked beans, butter beans, or mushrooms; the latter are best fried first for just a few minutes in butter.
Less stock and a can of tomatoes.
A sliced pimento, a few tablespoons of sherry and some frozen peas 30 minutes before end of cooking.

Pot-roasted beef

Imperial/Metric	American
3 lb./1¼ kg. topside or thick flank of beef	3 lb. chuck, rump or round of beef
2 oz./50 g. margarine	¼ cup margarine
1 tablespoon corn oil	1 tablespoon corn oil
1 onion, chopped	1 onion, chopped
2 large carrots, sliced	2 large carrots, sliced
2 large stalks celery, chopped	2 large stalks celery, chopped
2 teaspoons tomato purée	2 teaspoons tomato paste
½ pint/3 dl. stock or water	1¼ cups stock or water
1 tablespoon wine vinegar (optional)	1 tablespoon wine vinegar (optional)
salt and pepper	salt and pepper
12 small whole onions (optional)	12 small whole onions (optional)

Brown the joint briskly in the hot margarine and oil in a flameproof casserole. Remove the meat. Add the onion, carrots and celery and fry gently until golden. Replace the beef on top of the vegetables and add the tomato purée, stock, wine vinegar if used, and salt and pepper. Bring to the boil, lower the heat, and cover the pan tightly. Simmer very gently for 1 hour, turning at least twice. Add the whole onions and continue to simmer for about 30 minutes or until the meat is tender. Serve sliced with the vegetables and gravy from the pan.

Cooking time about 1½ hours

Minced beef for pies

This is a very basic mixture to be pepped up as you like with herbs, Worcestershire sauce, O.K. sauce, mushrooms or green pepper.

Imperial/Metric	American
1 medium-sized onion	1 medium-sized onion
2 rashers bacon	2 slices bacon
2 tablespoons oil	3 tablespoons oil
1 lb./450 g. minced beef	1 lb. ground beef
1 small can tomatoes	1 small can tomatoes
1 beef stock cube	1 beef bouillon cube
¾ pint/4 dl. water	2 cups water
1 tablespoon cornflour	1 tablespoon cornstarch
salt and pepper	salt and pepper

Peel and chop the onion. Remove the rind from the bacon and chop. Heat the oil in a large saucepan, add the bacon, onion and meat and stir until the meat has lost its pink colour. Add the tomatoes, stock cube and the water. Blend the cornflour with a little water, stir into the saucepan and bring the mixture to the boil, stirring continuously. Season, cover and simmer for 30 minutes. Cover with mashed potato and make a shepherd's pie; or cool the meat mixture, line a pie dish with shortcrust pastry, pour in the meat and cover with more pastry and bake in a moderately hot oven (400°F., 200°C., Gas Mark 6) for approximately 30 minutes.

Add ¼ pint (1½ dl., ⅔ cup) more water and a small can of tomato purée, plus whichever herbs you like, and you have a meat sauce for noodles or pasta.

Cooking time 30 minutes

Meatball casserole

Imperial/Metric	American
1 lb./450 g. minced beef	1 lb. ground beef
2 oz./50 g. fresh breadcrumbs	1 cup fresh bread crumbs
dash Worcestershire sauce	dash Worcestershire sauce
salt and pepper	salt and pepper
1 egg	1 egg
1 oz./25 g. flour	¼ cup flour
oil	oil
1 large onion	1 large onion
1 clove garlic (optional)	1 clove garlic (optional)
8 oz./225 g. carrots	½ lb. carrots
1 lb./450 g. potatoes	1 lb. potatoes
1 15-oz./425-g. can tomatoes	1 15-oz. can tomatoes
good pinch mixed herbs	good pinch mixed herbs
1 bay leaf	1 bay leaf
1 pint/6 dl. beef stock made with 1 stock cube and water	2½ cups beef stock made with 1 bouillon cube and water
chopped parsley	chopped parsley

Mix together the minced beef, breadcrumbs, Worcestershire sauce, salt, pepper, and lightly beaten egg. Form into balls and toss in the flour. Heat the oil and fry the meatballs until they are a light brown. Remove and put in a casserole. Chop the onion and fry lightly with the chopped garlic if used and add to the casserole with the sliced carrots. Cut the potatoes into 1-inch (2½-cm.) cubes, add to the casserole with the tomatoes, mixed herbs, bay leaf and stock. Season. Cook in a moderate oven for 1 hour. Sprinkle with chopped parsley.

Cooking time 1 hour
Oven temperature 350°F., 180°C., Gas Mark 4

Meat loaf

As with stew there are endless variations. It is such a useful dish as it is good both hot and cold, and the remains can be chopped up, mixed with a little tomato sauce, then poured over pasta to make a quick hot meal for the children. It pays to use good quality mince.

Imperial/Metric	American
1 onion	1 onion
1 egg	1 egg
2 sprigs parsley	2 sprigs parsley
salt and pepper	salt and pepper
2 thick slices bread	2 thick slices bread
little milk	little milk
1½ lb./675 g. minced beef	1½ lb. ground beef
tomato sauce	tomato sauce
1 oz./25 g. butter	2 tablespoons butter
3 tablespoons tomato purée	¼ cup tomato paste
¼ pint/1½ dl. water	⅔ cup water
pinch mixed herbs	pinch mixed herbs
salt and pepper	salt and pepper

Roughly chop the onion, then blend for a few seconds with the egg, parsley and seasoning. Remove the crusts from the bread, break into small pieces and soak in a little milk. Mix together the bread, meat and egg mixture and combine thoroughly. Shape the mixture into a loaf and place in a lightly greased roasting tin. Cover loosely with foil and bake in a moderately hot oven for 1 hour. To make the sauce, melt the butter, then blend in the purée and water, add herbs and seasonings. Remove the foil from the meat, pour the sauce over and return to the oven for 10 minutes.
Cooking time 1 hour 10 minutes
Oven temperature 375°F., 190°C., Gas Mark 5

Variations
Add 1–2 cloves garlic chopped with the onion and 1 teaspoon chilli powder or made mustard to sauce.
Put half the mixture in a loaf tin, place two hard-boiled eggs on it and cover with rest of mixture.
Cook in a loaf tin lined with flattened rashers of streaky bacon, using a rolling pin.
Cook the loaf for 40 minutes only, then wrap in puff pastry, increase the oven temperature to 400°F., 200°C., Gas Mark 6 and cook the loaf for a further 30 minutes.
A children's favourite Cook the loaf as above for 45 minutes, remove from the oven and let stand for 10 minutes. Pour off juices; place loaf in a shallow ovenproof dish. Cover with mashed potato, mark with a fork and return to the oven to brown.

Beef Louisiana

Imperial/Metric	American
4 rashers streaky bacon	4 slices bacon
1 lb./450 g. chuck steak	1 lb. chuck steak
oil	oil
1 large onion	1 large onion
½ green pepper (optional)	½ green pepper (optional)
1 clove garlic, crushed	1 clove garlic, crushed
½ teaspoon chilli powder	½ teaspoon chili powder
1 10½-oz./298-g. can tomato soup	1 10½-oz. can tomato soup

Fry the bacon until crisp, drain on a paper towel and crumble. Cut the meat into long strips, seal and brown in the bacon fat, adding a little oil if necessary. Stir in the sliced onion and pepper, the garlic and chilli. Cook for 5 minutes, then add the soup and bacon, cover and cook in a moderate oven until the meat is tender.
Cooking time 1½ hours
Oven temperature 325°F., 160°C., Gas Mark 3
Illustrated on page 27

Stuffed marrow

Imperial/Metric	American
1 medium-sized marrow	1 medium-sized marrow squash or 2 large zucchini
stuffing	stuffing
1 tablespoon oil	1 tablespoon oil
1 lb./450 g. minced beef	1 lb. ground beef
1 large onion, chopped	1 large onion, chopped
2 tablespoons long-grain rice	3 tablespoons long-grain rice
1 tablespoon tomato purée	1 tablespoon tomato paste
1 clove garlic or garlic salt	1 clove garlic or garlic salt
3–4 oz./75–100 g. raisins or sultanas	½–⅔ cup dark or white seedless raisins
large pinch mixed herbs	large pinch mixed herbs
salt and pepper	salt and pepper
½ pint/3 dl. beef stock made with 1 stock cube and water	1¼ cups beef stock made with 1 bouillon cube and water

To make the stuffing, heat the oil in a frying pan and fry the meat until well browned. Remove the meat and add the onion and rice to the frying pan; fry until the rice is transparent. Add the meat, tomato purée, garlic, raisins, herbs, and salt and pepper. Gradually add the stock and bring to the boil, stirring all the time. Simmer gently for 20 minutes.

Meanwhile cut the marrow into rings about 2 inches (5 cm.) wide and remove the seeds. Do not peel the marrow as the peel helps to prevent the rings falling apart. Place the rings on a baking dish and pile the stuffing in the middle of each ring. Pour a little oil into the dish and cook in a moderately hot oven for about 1 hour, or until the marrow is really tender. After half an hour it may be necessary to cover the rings with a sheet of foil to prevent the meat burning.

Cooking time about 1 hour
Oven temperature 375°F., 190°C., Gas Mark 5

Lamb

Chops
Try chopping a little mint, mixing with some butter to a smooth cream, forming into pats and chilling. Serve one on each grilled chop.
Grill chops with a few slivers of garlic inserted in the meat or at least a sprinkling of garlic salt and some rosemary.
Trim off excess fat, dip chops in breadcrumbs, then beaten egg then crumbs again and fry.

Roast
As a change from serving roast lamb with mint sauce, try spreading the following mixture over the meat an hour before cooking, then serving with a simple pilaff (see page 39). For a roast weighing approximately 3 lb. (1¼ kg.), put a good teaspoon of French mustard in a small bowl, slowly add 2 tablespoons oil and stir until thick. Add a crushed garlic clove, salt, pepper, 1 tablespoon soy sauce and 1 teaspoon ginger.

Lamb and mushroom pie

Imperial/Metric	American
12 oz./350 g. leftover lamb from joint	3 cups leftover lamb from roast
1 small onion	1 small onion
½ pint/3 dl. lamb gravy	1¼ cups lamb gravy
2–4 oz./50–100 g. mushrooms	½–1 cup mushrooms
1½ lb./675 g. mashed potatoes	3 cups mashed potatoes

Mince the lamb and the onion together and mix with the gravy. Slice the mushrooms thinly and add to

the lamb. Put in the base of a pie dish and top with the mashed potatoes. Cook in a moderate oven for about 30 minutes.
Cooking time 30 minutes
Oven temperature 350°F., 180°C., Gas Mark 4

Breast of lamb sandwich

This is a very cheap and filling meal.

Imperial/Metric	American
2 breasts of lamb, boned	2 breasts of lamb, boned
stuffing	stuffing
8 oz./225 g. sausage meat	1 cup sausage meat
2 tablespoons dry sage and onion stuffing mix	3 tablespoons dry sage and onion stuffing mix
½ teaspoon mixed herbs	½ teaspoon mixed herbs
salt and pepper	salt and pepper

Mix all the stuffing ingredients together in a bowl. Place one of the breasts, boned side uppermost, in a baking tin. Spread thickly with the stuffing and lay the second breast on top, with the boned side to the stuffing. Tie the sandwich with string to prevent it from curling and roast it in a moderate oven for 40 minutes per lb. (½ kg.).
Cooking time 40 minutes per lb. (½ kg.)
Oven temperature 350°F., 180°C., Gas Mark 4

Lamb chops in casserole

Imperial/Metric	American
6 small lamb chops	6 small lamb chops
12 baby onions, or 3 large onions, quartered	12 baby onions, or 3 large onions, quartered
4 oz./100 g. mushrooms	1 cup mushrooms
pinch herbs	pinch herbs
salt and pepper	salt and pepper
1 large can baked beans	1 large can baked beans

Fry the chops quickly for 1 minute on each side, just to brown them. Place them in a casserole, side by side. Add the onions, mushrooms, herbs, and a little salt and pepper. Pour the baked beans over and cover the casserole. Cook in a moderate oven for 40 minutes.
Cooking time 40 minutes
Oven temperature 350°F., 180°C., Gas Mark 4
Illustrated on page 27

Cold minted lamb chops

Imperial/Metric	American
4 lamb chops	4 lamb chops
oil	oil
2 large sprigs mint, finely chopped	2 large sprigs mint, finely chopped
1 lemon	1 lemon
½ teaspoon castor sugar	½ teaspoon granulated sugar
salt and pepper	salt and pepper
½ cucumber	½ cucumber
1 tablespoon parsley	1 tablespoon parsley

Preheat the grill. Trim the excess fat from the chops, then brush with oil and cook for approximately 15 minutes or until tender. Drain on absorbent paper and put in a dish with the mint, juice from half the lemon, sugar, 2 tablespoons oil, and salt and pepper. Mix well, then leave the chops to cool, turning a few times. Thinly slice the cucumber and arrange on a serving plate. Put the cold chops on the top and spoon over the liquid, sprinkle on the parsley and garnish with lemon wedges. Serve with a simple cold potato salad or new potatoes.

Cooking time 15 minutes

Pork and bacon

One of the best pork joints to buy is a boned and rolled hand. They are generally quite large, but cold pork is delicious and useful, and it is a joint which butchers often eat themselves – a good sign! To make the crackling really crisp, rub it well with a mixture of 1 tablespoon each of salt and oil, and don't baste the fat for the last 40 minutes. As an alternative, rub in a mixture of salt, black pepper, thyme, crushed bay leaf and garlic, and leave for several hours before cooking. Peeled apple rings fried in butter make a good alternative to apple sauce.

Pot-roasted blade of pork

Imperial/Metric	American
1 pork blade or spare rib joint	1 blade loin roast of pork or loin roast
oil	oil
1 large onion	1 large onion
2 carrots	2 carrots
1 clove garlic	1 clove garlic
¼ pint/1½ dl. wine or stock with 2 tablespoons wine vinegar added	⅔ cup wine or stock with 3 tablespoons wine vinegar added
salt and pepper	salt and pepper
potatoes (optional)	potatoes (optional)

Score the rind of the pork, heat the oil in a heavy casserole and fry the meat to brown it all over. Remove the meat. Dice the onion and carrots and chop the garlic, fry for a few minutes. Place the meat on top of the vegetables with the rind uppermost, and pour over the liquid. Season and cover the casserole. Cook in a moderate oven allowing 30 minutes per lb. (½ kg.). Potatoes cooked in the pot for the last half hour will save another saucepan to wash and give the potatoes a delicious flavour. If your family like lots of gravy, strain the juices, thicken with flour and add more stock.

Cooking time 30 minutes per lb. (½ kg.)
Oven temperature 350°F., 180°C., Gas Mark 4

Pork patties

Imperial/Metric	American
8 oz./225 g. minced cooked pork	1 cup ground cooked pork
4 oz./100 g. minced bacon	½ cup ground bacon
4 oz./100 g. fresh breadcrumbs	2 cups fresh bread crumbs
½ teaspoon sage or mixed herbs	½ teaspoon sage or mixed herbs
1 egg	1 egg
¼ pint/1½ dl. milk	⅔ cup milk
salt and pepper	salt and pepper
quick tomato sauce (see page 15)	quick tomato sauce (see page 15)
or	or
mustard sauce	mustard sauce
½ pint/3 dl. white sauce	1¼ cups white sauce
salt and pepper	salt and pepper
2 teaspoons dry mustard	2 teaspoons dry mustard
2 teaspoons vinegar	2 teaspoons vinegar

Mix together the pork, bacon, breadcrumbs and sage or herbs. Beat the egg and milk together and add to the meat mixture, season and turn the mixture on to a floured board. Divide into eight and shape each piece into a thick cake. Place in a heatproof dish and put into a moderately hot oven for 10 minutes. To make the mustard sauce, add to the white sauce the salt and pepper to taste and the mustard mixed with the vinegar. Pour the chosen sauce over the patties and return to the oven for 15 minutes.

Cooking time 25 minutes
Oven temperature 375°F., 190°C., Gas Mark 5

Resurrection pork

Imperial/Metric	American
10–12 oz./275–350 g. cooked pork	2–3 cups cooked pork
1 medium-sized onion	1 medium-sized onion
pork dripping or oil	pork drippings or oil
garlic salt (optional)	garlic salt (optional)
1 10-oz./283-g. can condensed mushroom soup	1 10-oz. can condensed mushroom soup
¼ soup can water	¼ soup can water
2 teaspoons Worcestershire sauce	2 teaspoons Worcestershire sauce
little Tabasco or red pepper (optional)	little Tabasco or red pepper (optional)
salt and pepper	salt and pepper
4 oz./100 g. mushrooms (optional)	1 cup mushrooms (optional)

Cut the meat into small thin pieces trimming off most of the fat. Peel and chop the onion, heat the dripping or oil and fry the onion until golden. Put the meat and onion into a casserole, sprinkle on the garlic salt if liked and pour over the soup, water, Worcestershire sauce, Tabasco, salt and pepper. Mix well and cover. Cook in a moderately hot oven for 30 minutes, with the addition, just before serving, of the mushrooms, thinly sliced and fried in a little butter. Serve in a shallow dish surrounded by mashed potato or rice.

Cooking time 30 minutes
Oven temperature 375°F., 190°C., Gas Mark 5

Pork and beans

A very quick and easy to make version, good for a cold day.

Imperial/Metric	American
1 lb./450 g. belly of pork	1 lb. fresh pork picnic shoulder
2 medium-sized onions	2 medium-sized onions
1 clove garlic (optional)	1 clove garlic (optional)
1 large can tomatoes	1 large can tomatoes
1 large can baked beans	1 large can baked beans
salt and pepper	salt and pepper

Cut the meat into small square pieces, trimming off any pieces of bone and some of the fat. Put in a large casserole and fry gently for 10 minutes, then remove and keep warm. Slice the onions and fry until they are soft and golden; add the chopped garlic if used. Return the pork to the casserole, add the tomatoes, chopping them a little as you add them. Stir in the beans, season well, cover and bake in a moderate oven for 40–50 minutes, or until the meat is tender. Serve with lots of mashed potato or potatoes in their jackets.

Cooking time 40–50 minutes
Oven temperature 350°F., 180°C., Gas Mark 4

Ham beehive

Imperial/Metric	American
12 oz.–1 lb./350–450 g. cooked bacon	1½–2 cups ground ham
1½ oz./40 g. margarine	3 tablespoons margarine
1½ oz./40 g. flour	6 tablespoons flour
½ pint/3 dl. milk	1¼ cups milk
2 eggs	2 eggs
pepper	pepper
made mustard	made mustard
2 lb./900 g. mashed potatoes	4 cups mashed potatoes
quick tomato sauce	quick tomato sauce
2 tablespoons tomato purée	3 tablespoons tomato paste
¼ pint/1½ dl. water	⅔ cup water
pinch herbs	pinch herbs
garlic salt and pepper	garlic salt and pepper

Trim off the excess fat and mince the bacon coarsely. Make a white sauce with the margarine, flour and milk and cook for 1–2 minutes. Beat in the eggs, reserving a little for glazing. Fold the sauce into the bacon and season. Turn the mixture into a greased 2-pint (1-litre, 5-cup) pudding basin and cover with a piece of greased greaseproof paper and then with foil. Place the bowl in a baking tin with about 1 inch (2½ cm.) water in it. Cook in a moderately hot oven for 1½ hours. Turn out on to a heatproof plate, leaving the basin on for a few minutes to allow the mould to settle. Completely mask with the mashed potatoes and smooth with a palette knife. Mark the surface in 'scallops' with a damp spoon handle. Return to a hot oven for 10 minutes. Remove from the oven, brush with beaten egg, and return to the oven until golden.

To make the quick tomato sauce, mix all the ingredients together and bring to the boil, stirring. Simmer for 2–3 minutes. Serve with the hot ham beehive.

Cooking time about 1¾ hours
Oven temperature 375°F., 190°C., Gas Mark 5, then 450°F., 230°C., Gas Mark 8

15

Foil-roasted bacon joint

Imperial/Metric	American
3 lb./1¼ kg. unsmoked bacon hock joint	3 lb. ham shank or butt
1 teaspoon made mustard	1 teaspoon made mustard
2 teaspoons soft brown sugar	2 teaspoons soft brown sugar
salt and pepper	salt and pepper

Place the joint in a large piece of foil and wrap up tightly. Stand the parcel in a baking tin half full of boiling water. Cook in a moderate oven for 1¼ hours. There is no need to baste the joint at all, but top up the water if necessary. After 1¼ hours remove the bacon from the foil and peel off the thick rind. Pour the water in the tin away. Mark the fat into squares with a sharp knife. Mix together the mustard, sugar, salt and pepper and smooth over the fat. Put in a hot oven in the dry tin for 15 minutes until the fat is crisp and brown. Serve hot or cold.

Cooking time 1½ hours
Oven temperature 350°F., 180°C., Gas Mark 4, then 425°F., 220°C., Gas Mark 7

Bacon plait

This is a very useful recipe for the end of the month, when the housekeeping is running out! It is also good cold for picnics.

Imperial/Metric	American
8 oz./225 g. shortcrust pastry or 8 oz./225 g. pastry mix	basic pie dough made with 2 cups flour or 1 8-oz. stick pie crust mix
4 oz./100 g. streaky bacon or bacon bits	¼ lb. bacon slices
3 tomatoes	3 tomatoes
parsley, thyme or any other herbs you have	parsley, thyme or any other herbs you have
salt and pepper	salt and pepper
little milk or beaten egg to glaze	little milk or beaten egg to glaze

Roll out the pastry to an 11-inch (23-cm.) square and place on a baking tin. Chop up the bacon roughly; skin and chop the tomatoes and mix with the bacon. Add herbs and salt and pepper. Put the filling in a 3-inch (7-cm.) band down the centre of the pastry. Make diagonal cuts at ½-inch (1-cm.) intervals from the filling to the edge of the pastry on either side. Lay the strips alternately from either side across the filling and tuck in the ends to neaten.

Brush the top with egg or milk, then bake in a moderately hot oven for 30–40 minutes, when the top should be golden brown.

Cooking time 30–40 minutes
Oven temperature 400°F., 200°C., Gas Mark 6
Illustrated on page 59

Bacon and potato hotpot

Imperial/Metric	American
2 oz./50 g. margarine or butter	¼ cup margarine or butter
2 oz./50 g. flour	½ cup flour
1 pint/6 dl. milk	2½ cups milk
bay leaf	bay leaf
salt and pepper	salt and pepper
3 large onions, or 1 onion and 3 leeks	3 large onions, or 1 onion and 3 leeks
4 large potatoes	4 large potatoes
8 oz./225 g. bacon pieces or streaky rashers	½ lb. bacon slices
2 oz./50 g. cheese, grated	½ cup grated cheese

Melt the margarine, stir in the flour and add the cold milk, stirring until the sauce boils and thickens. Add the bay leaf and salt and pepper. Leave to simmer gently. Meanwhile, peel the onions and potatoes and slice thinly; cut the bacon into strips with scissors. Grease a large casserole and fill with alternate layers of onion, potato and bacon, ending with potato. Remove the bay leaf from the sauce and pour over the casserole, giving it a shake to distribute the sauce evenly. Cover and bake in a moderate oven for 1 hour. Remove the lid and bake for a further hour. Half an hour before the end of the cooking time sprinkle the grated cheese over the top.

This can also be made with leftover ham if you like.

Cooking time 2 hours
Oven temperature 350°F., 180°C., Gas Mark 4

Sausage tart

Imperial/Metric	American
pinch dried mixed herbs	pinch dried mixed herbs
8 oz./225 g. pork sausage meat	1 cup pork sausage meat
1 7- to 8-inch shortcrust pastry case, uncooked	1 basic pie shell, unbaked
2 eggs	2 eggs
1 tablespoon milk	1 tablespoon milk
5 oz. cooked peas	1 cup cooked peas
salt and pepper	salt and pepper

Mix the herbs into the sausage meat and spread over the base of the pastry, leaving a hollow in the centre. Beat the eggs and milk together, add the well-drained cooked peas, salt and pepper, and pour over the sausage meat. Bake for 35–40 minutes in a moderately hot oven and serve hot or cold. This makes ideal picnic food.

Cooking time 35–40 minutes

Oven temperature 400°F., 200°C., Gas Mark 6

Illustrated on page 59

Stuffed frankfurters

Imperial/Metric	American
1 onion	1 onion
1 green pepper (optional)	1 green sweet pepper (optional)
oil	oil
1 can baked beans	1 can baked beans
1 small can tomatoes	1 small can tomatoes
salt and pepper	salt and pepper
1 lb./450 g. frankfurters	1 lb. frankfurters
little made mustard	little made mustard
3 oz./75 g. Cheddar cheese, grated	¾ cup grated Cheddar cheese
Worcestershire sauce	Worcestershire sauce

Chop the onion and pepper and fry in a little oil until soft. Put into a shallow ovenproof dish and add the baked beans, chopped tomatoes and seasoning. Make a lengthwise slit in the sausages, spread with mustard and fill with grated cheese. Put the sausages on top of the vegetables, sprinkle with a little Worcestershire sauce and cook in a moderate oven for 30 minutes. Finish under the grill to brown cheese if necessary. Jacket potatoes and a green salad are all you need with this dish.

Cooking time 30 minutes

Oven temperature 350°F., 180°C., Gas Mark 4

Illustrated on page 27

Liver and kidneys

As a change from liver and bacon try the following ways of cooking liver:

Cut the liver in very small pieces, then add to a pan of soft, golden fried onions with a little wine vinegar and lemon juice.

Spread large slices of liver with French mustard before frying.

Liver is also improved if you leave it to marinate in a little wine vinegar or lemon juice before cooking. Leaving the liver to soak for an hour or two in milk will make the flavour milder and more acceptable to children.

Braised liver

A delicious way of cooking liver and, odd as they seem, do not be tempted to leave out the cloves. The lemon is also important.

Imperial/Metric	American
1 onion	1 onion
2 carrots	2 carrots
oil	oil
1 oz./25 g. fresh breadcrumbs	½ cup fresh bread crumbs
1 lb./450 g. lamb's liver, sliced	1 lb. lamb liver, sliced
1 15-oz./425-g. can tomatoes	1 15-oz. can tomatoes
1 teaspoon dried sage	1 teaspoon dried sage
4 cloves	4 cloves
1 clove garlic	1 clove garlic
salt and pepper	salt and pepper
4 slices white bread	4 slices white bread
chopped parsley	chopped parsley
1 lemon	1 lemon

Finely slice the onion and carrots. Heat a little oil and lightly fry the vegetables and breadcrumbs; add the liver and fry for 1 minute on each side. Add the tomatoes, sage, cloves, finely chopped garlic, salt and pepper; add cold water almost to cover the liver and bring to the boil. Lower the heat, cover the pan and cook until the liver is tender. This will depend on the thickness of the slices. Fry the slices of bread until crisp and serve the liver with triangles of fried bread, chopped parsley and slices of lemon.

Cooking time 20–30 minutes

Savoury kidneys

Imperial/Metric	American
6 lamb's kidneys, more if they are a favourite	6 lamb kidneys, more if they are a favorite
1 teaspoon vinegar	1 teaspoon vinegar
2 onions	2 onions
2 oz./50 g. butter	¼ cup butter
4 oz./100 g. mushrooms	1 cup mushrooms
1 tablespoon flour	1 tablespoon flour
1 teaspoon tomato purée	1 teaspoon tomato paste
½ pint/3 dl. stock made with 1 stock cube and water	1¼ cups stock made with 1 bouillon cube and water
2 tablespoons sherry (optional)	3 tablespoons sherry (optional)
salt and pepper	salt and pepper
bay leaf	bay leaf

Skin the kidneys and rinse in water with the vinegar. Cut in half lengthwise, remove the core and slice. Thinly slice the onions. Heat the butter and sauté the onions for 10 minutes, remove and keep warm. Sauté the kidneys for 3 minutes, then add the thinly sliced mushrooms. Heat through, stir in the flour and purée, slowly add the stock and sherry then the seasonings and bay leaf. Bring to the boil, return the onions to the pan and simmer till the kidneys are tender. Serve in a ring of mashed potatoes or rice.
Cooking time about 25 minutes

Liver and bacon provençal

Imperial/Metric	American
1 lb./450 g. lamb's liver	1 lb. lamb liver
2 oz./50 g. flour	½ cup flour
2 tablespoons oil	3 tablespoons oil
4 oz./100 g. streaky bacon, chopped	5 slices bacon, chopped
3 medium-sized onions	3 medium-sized onions
1 14-oz./397-g. can tomatoes	1 14-oz. can tomatoes
½ teaspoon marjoram or thyme	½ teaspoon marjoram or thyme
1 bay leaf	1 bay leaf
1 tablespoon Worcestershire sauce	1 tablespoon Worcestershire sauce
¼ pint/1½ dl. chicken stock	⅔ cup chicken stock
salt and pepper	salt and pepper

Slice the liver into long thick strips and coat with the flour. Fry in the oil until golden brown. Place in a casserole. Add the bacon and the sliced onions to the frying pan and cook until golden. Stir in the remainder of the flour in which the liver was dipped. Add the tomatoes, herbs and Worcestershire sauce. Stir in the stock, season well and pour into the casserole. Cover and cook in a moderate oven for about 30 minutes. Serve with plain boiled potatoes and a salad.
Cooking time 30 minutes
Oven temperature 350°F., 180°C., Gas Mark 4

Liver and mushrooms with herbs

This is a delicious dish, but it is rather rich, so don't give the children too large a helping.

Imperial/Metric	American
1 lb./450 g. lamb's liver, cut into thin strips	1 lb. lamb liver, cut into thin strips
½ pint/3 dl. milk	1¼ cups milk
2 tablespoons seasoned flour	3 tablespoons seasoned flour
2 oz./50 g. butter	¼ cup butter
8 oz./225 g. mushrooms, sliced	2 cups sliced mushrooms
1–2 tablespoons finely chopped mixed parsley and chives	1–2 tablespoons finely chopped mixed parsley and chives
juice of ½ lemon	juice of ½ lemon

Put the liver into a bowl and cover with milk. Allow to soak for 1 hour, then drain well. Add the seasoned flour to the bowl and stir to cover the liver. Melt the butter in a frying pan and brown the liver quickly all over. Reduce the heat and add the sliced mushrooms and the parsley and chives. Cover, and cook gently for 4–5 minutes, shaking occasionally. Pour the lemon juice over, and serve with new potatoes.
Cooking time 10–15 minutes

Cheese and bacon loaf (page 41) and mixed vegetable soup (page 5)

Chicken and game

Brunswick stew

Imperial/Metric	American
1 3-lb./1¼-kg. stewing or roasting chicken	1 3-lb. stewing or roasting chicken
2 teaspoons salt	2 teaspoons salt
bay leaf	bay leaf
1 medium-sized onion, chopped	1 medium-sized onion, chopped
1 oz./25 g. butter	2 tablespoons butter
1 large can tomatoes	1 large can tomatoes
salt and black pepper	salt and black pepper
1 tablespoon dried or fresh parsley	1 tablespoon dried or fresh parsley
1 tablespoon Worcestershire sauce	1 tablespoon Worcestershire sauce
little lemon peel	little lemon peel
1 teaspoon sugar	1 teaspoon sugar
1 7-oz./198-g. can sweetcorn	1 7-oz. can corn
1 can broad beans	1 can lima beans
1½ oz./40 g. flour	⅓ cup flour
6 tablespoons water	½ cup water

Cover the chicken with water, add the salt and bay leaf and simmer for about 1 hour, or until the chicken is tender. Remove the chicken from the bone, reserving a scant ¾ pint (4 dl., 1¾ cups) of the stock. Cut the chicken into bite-sized pieces. In a large saucepan sauté the onion in the butter. When soft add the tomatoes, seasoning, herbs, sauce, peel, sugar and stock. Simmer for 20 minutes; add the chicken, corn and beans and simmer for 30 minutes. Mix the flour and water to a smooth paste and stir into the stew. Continue cooking until the stew has thickened.
Cooking time about 2½ hours

French roast chicken

This is a marvellous way of roasting a chicken, as it keeps the chicken beautifully moist inside but with a crisp brown skin.

Imperial/Metric	American
1 3½- to 4-lb./1½- to 1¾-kg. roasting chicken with giblets	1 3½- to 4-lb. roasting chicken with giblets
1 small onion	1 small onion
salt and pepper	salt and pepper
2 oz./50 g. butter	¼ cup butter
1 tablespoon cream	1 tablespoon cream

First remove the liver from the giblets and set aside. Cover the rest of the giblets with water, add the sliced onion, some salt and pepper and bring to the boil. Simmer for 30 minutes and drain off the resulting stock into a baking tin. Put the chicken into the tin with a knob of butter inside and on top and baste with the stock. Put into a moderately hot oven and after 20 minutes turn the chicken on to one side, and on to the other side after a further 20 minutes. Baste with the stock frequently. You will find that the chicken will be cooked in 1 hour using this method. Remove the chicken and keep it hot. Chop the liver and fry gently for 1 minute in a little butter. Add to the chicken stock with 1 tablespoon cream and serve as gravy.
Cooking time 1 hour
Oven temperature 375°F., 190°C., Gas Mark 5

Chicken Majorca

Imperial/Metric	American
1 8-oz./227-g. packet savoury rice or tomato rice	1 cup seasoned rice or tomato rice
1 small can tomatoes	1 small can tomatoes
1 oz./25 g. chopped walnuts	3 tablespoons chopped walnuts
8 stuffed olives (optional)	8 stuffed olives (optional)
1 roasting chicken, about 3 lb./1¼ kg.	1 roasting chicken, about 3 lb.
1 oz./25 g. butter	2 tablespoons butter
½ pint/3 dl. unsweetened orange juice, canned or frozen	1¼ cups unsweetened orange juice, canned or frozen
1 tablespoon flour	1 tablespoon flour
2 tablespoons cold water	3 tablespoons cold water
salt and pepper	salt and pepper
little wine or sherry (optional)	little wine or sherry (optional)

Slightly undercook the rice and mix with the drained and chopped tomatoes and walnuts, plus, if you like the flavour, the olives, chopped. Mix well and spoon into the chicken. (If there is any rice over, save it to use mixed with a little tuna fish and put into hollowed out tomatoes, which you bake.) Put the chicken in a baking tin and spread the butter over the breast. Pour the orange juice over the chicken and roast in a moderately hot oven, basting frequently with the juices. When the chicken is tender put on a carving dish and keep warm. Mix the flour and water until smooth, add to the pan

juices and slowly bring to the boil, stirring; simmer for a few minutes, taste for seasoning, then serve with the chicken. To make a richer sauce, add a little wine or sherry with the flour.
Cooking time 1½–1¾ hours
Oven temperature 400°F., 200°C., Gas Mark 6

Austrian chicken pancakes

Imperial/Metric	American
pancakes	pancakes
2 eggs	**2 eggs**
3 oz./75 g. plain flour	**¾ cup all-purpose flour**
½ pint/3 dl. milk	**1¼ cups milk**
1 oz./25 g. butter, melted	**2 tablespoons melted butter**
chicken mixture	chicken mixture
1 oz./25 g. butter	**2 tablespoons butter**
2 tablespoons lemon juice	**3 tablespoons lemon juice**
12 oz./350 g. cooked chicken, diced	**2 cups cooked diced chicken**
4 oz./100 g. mushrooms, chopped	**1 cup chopped mushrooms**
salt and pinch cayenne pepper	**salt and pinch cayenne pepper**
1 teaspoon flour creamed with knob of butter	**1 teaspoon flour creamed with knob of butter**
2 tablespoons top of the milk	**3 tablespoons half and half**
Parmesan cheese	**Parmesan cheese**

Make a smooth batter by mixing the eggs with the flour and slowly adding the milk. Leave to stand for at least 1 hour. Make four pancakes by heating a little of the butter, pouring in the batter, cooking until starting to brown, then tossing or turning with a palette knife. Cook the same way on the other side. Remove from the pan and put the pancakes on a wire mesh tray.

To make the chicken mixture, melt the butter over a low flame, add the lemon juice and chicken, cover and cook for a few minutes. Stir in the mushrooms, salt and pepper, cook for a few more minutes, then stir in the creamed flour and butter and the milk. Cook for 5 minutes more. Spoon equal quantities of the chicken mixture on to each pancake, roll up and place the pancakes on a shallow heatproof dish. Sprinkle with Parmesan cheese and brown for a few minutes in a hot oven.
Cooking time pancakes few minutes, filling about 15 minutes
Oven temperature 425°F., 220°C., Gas Mark 7

Monica's chicken casserole

This is a useful recipe for the weekend as everything goes into one pot which cuts down the washing up.

Imperial/Metric	American
4 chicken joints	**4 chicken pieces**
1 oz./25 g. butter	**2 tablespoons butter**
2 onions, sliced	**2 onions, sliced**
4 carrots, sliced	**4 carrots, sliced**
1 can cream of chicken soup	**1 can cream of chicken soup**
4 potatoes, thinly sliced	**4 potatoes, thinly sliced**
salt and pepper	**salt and pepper**

Brown the chicken joints in the butter and put into a casserole. Cover with sliced onions and carrots and pour the soup over. Arrange overlapping slices of potato on top, add seasoning and cover with a lid. Cook in a moderate oven for 1 hour. Remove the lid and cook for a further 30 minutes.
Cooking time 1½ hours
Oven temperature 350°F., 180°C., Gas Mark 4

Chicken casserole mix

This can be used as given below or as a base for a pie or cobbler, see variations.

Imperial/Metric	American
1 chicken, about 3 lb./ 1¼ kg., cut into 8 pieces	**1 chicken, about 3 lb., cut into 8 pieces**
2 carrots	**2 carrots**
2 medium-sized onions	**2 medium-sized onions**
4 oz./100 g. mushrooms	**1 cup mushrooms**
2 stalks celery	**2 stalks celery**
1½ oz./40 g. margarine	**3 tablespoons margarine**
1½ oz./40 g. flour	**6 tablespoons flour**
½ pint/3 dl. milk	**1¼ cups milk**
½ pint/3 dl. chicken stock or water and stock cube	**1¼ cups chicken stock or water and bouillon cube**
salt and pepper	**salt and pepper**

Wash and dry the chicken. Peel and slice the carrots and onions, wash and slice the mushrooms and celery. Melt the margarine in a large pan and fry the chicken quickly to brown; remove to a casserole. Fry the vegetables for 5 minutes, shaking the pan a few times, then put with the chicken. Stir the flour into the remaining fat (melt a little more if it has all disappeared), then slowly add the milk and stock, bring to the boil stirring continuously and simmer for 2 minutes. Pour over the chicken and vegetables, add seasoning, cover and cook for 1 hour in a moderate oven. Serve with mashed potatoes.

Cooking time 1 hour
Oven temperature 350°F., 180°C., Gas Mark 4

Variations
Chicken pie Cook the chicken for 30 minutes, then remove from the oven and cool. Raise the oven temperature to 425°F., 220°C., Gas Mark 7, cover the pie with puff pastry and cook for a further 30 minutes.
Chicken cobbler Cook the casserole for 40 minutes, then top with overlapping rounds of scone dough (see page 42) and cook uncovered in a hot oven (425°F., 220°C., Gas Mark 7) until the cobbler is golden brown, about 10–15 minutes.

Chicken salad

This can be made with cooked leftover chicken just as well. If you don't have much chicken, increase the number of hard-boiled eggs to pad the salad out a bit.

Imperial/Metric	American
4 chicken joints	4 chicken pieces
1 cucumber	1 cucumber
salt and black pepper	salt and black pepper
2 hard-boiled eggs	2 hard-cooked eggs
chopped chives	chopped chives
few gherkins (optional)	few dill pickles (optional)
dressing	dressing
5 tablespoons mayonnaise	6 tablespoons mayonnaise
3 tablespoons top of the milk	¼ cup half and half
1 tablespoon lemon juice	1 tablespoon lemon juice
1 teaspoon made English mustard	1 teaspoon made English mustard

First of all cook the chicken joints in a moderate oven for half an hour, with a knob of butter on top of each. Allow to cool, then remove all the meat and dice it.

Peel the cucumber and cut it in half lengthways. Remove the seeds and cut the flesh into small chunks. Put them into a saucepan and cover with cold water. Bring to the boil, remove from the heat, drain and allow to cool. Mix the cucumber and chicken together and put into a basin. Season well with salt and black pepper.

To make the dressing, combine all the ingredients together and pour over the chicken mixture. Pile

the whole lot on to a serving dish, garnish with sliced hard-boiled egg and sprinkle with finely chopped chives. Add chopped up gherkins if you like them. Serve with brown bread and butter.

Cooking time 30 minutes
Oven temperature 350°F., 180°C., Gas Mark 4

Fried chicken

This is one of the most useful ways of cooking chicken, delicious with fried potatoes and a salad, as chicken Maryland with corn fritters (see page 25) and fried bananas, or cold with a potato salad as perfect picnic food.

Imperial/Metric	American
1 small young chicken, jointed, or required number of chicken pieces	1 small young chicken, jointed, or required number of chicken pieces
2 tablespoons flour	3 tablespoons flour
salt, pepper and paprika	salt, pepper and paprika
1 egg, beaten (optional)	1 egg, beaten (optional)
crushed cornflakes or dry homemade breadcrumbs (optional)	crushed cornflakes or dry homemade bread crumbs (optional)
oil for frying	oil for frying

Wash and dry the chicken joints. Shake one piece at a time in a polythene bag, with the flour, salt, pepper and a little paprika. Put oil ½ inch (1 cm.) deep in a heavy frying pan and heat until hot but not smoking. Fry the chicken with just the flour coating or dip in the beaten egg and roll in cornflakes or crumbs. Fry skin side down until golden, turn, cook the other side then reduce the heat and cover. Tilt the lid so that the steam can escape. Cook for 30–40 minutes. Drain well on absorbent paper.

Cooking time 40–50 minutes

Salmon pie (page 9), apricot condé (page 28), Portuguese plaice (page 8) and pineapple and coconut sponge (page 47)

Lemon chicken casserole

The ingredients of this recipe may sound rather odd, but do try it as it is very quick and really delicious.

Imperial/Metric	American
1 3½- to 4-lb./1½- to 1¾-kg. roasting chicken or 4 chicken joints	1 3½- to 4-lb. roasting chicken or 4 chicken pieces
6 rashers streaky bacon, cut into small pieces	6 slices bacon, cut into small pieces
1 tablespoon white wine vinegar	1 tablespoon white wine vinegar
4 slices lemon	4 slices lemon
2 teaspoons capers	2 teaspoons capers
2 onions, sliced	2 onions, sliced
¼ pint/1½ dl. chicken stock	⅔ cup chicken stock
salt and pepper	salt and pepper

Place all the ingredients in a casserole. Cover with foil and a close fitting lid. Cook in a moderate oven for 1½ hours.
Cooking time 1½ hours
Oven temperature 350°F., 180°C., Gas Mark 4

Rabbit casserole

Imperial/Metric	American
1 rabbit, jointed	1 rabbit, jointed
little salt and vinegar	little salt and vinegar
8 oz./225 g. streaky bacon	½ lb. bacon
2 tablespoons dripping or oil	3 tablespoons drippings or oil
2 small onions, quartered	2 small onions, quartered
1 tablespoon flour	1 tablespoon flour
1 pint/6 dl. chicken stock made with 1 stock cube and water	2½ cups chicken stock made with 1 bouillon cube and water
pepper	pepper
bouquet garni or 1 teaspoon mixed herbs	bouquet garni or 1 teaspoon mixed herbs
few mushrooms (optional)	few mushrooms (optional)
2 tablespoons cream or top of the milk	3 tablespoons cream or half and half
2 teaspoons French mustard	2 teaspoons French mustard
2 teaspoons chopped parsley	2 teaspoons chopped parsley

Trim the rabbit joints and soak overnight in salted water with a little vinegar; this removes the strong rabbit flavour. Drain the joints, rinse and dry. Remove the rinds and roughly chop the bacon, blanch for 1 minute in boiling water, drain well. Heat the dripping or oil, lightly fry the rabbit, remove, fry the onions for a few minutes, add the bacon, stir in the flour, slowly add the stock and bring to the boil. Add the pepper, bouquet garni or herbs, mushrooms and the rabbit joints. Cover and cook in a moderate oven for about 1½ hours, or until the rabbit is really tender. Remove the bouquet garni. Mix the cream or top of the milk with the mustard and parsley and stir into the casserole. Reheat for a few minutes and serve with lots of mashed potato.
Cooking time about 1½ hours
Oven temperature 350°F., 180°C., Gas Mark 4

Curry sauce

This sauce can be used with any leftover meat. It also freezes well which is useful.

Imperial/Metric	American
1 oz./25 g. butter	2 tablespoons butter
1 tablespoon oil	1 tablespoon oil
1 onion, chopped	1 onion, chopped
1 apple, chopped	1 apple, chopped
2 teaspoons curry powder (or more)	2 teaspoons curry powder (or more)
1 oz./25 g. flour	¼ cup flour
salt and pepper	salt and pepper
½ bay leaf	½ bay leaf
1 clove garlic, crushed	1 clove garlic, crushed
1 pint/6 dl. stock	2½ cups stock
1 tablespoon chutney or plum jam	1 tablespoon chutney or plum jam
juice of ½ lemon	juice of ½ lemon
1 teaspoon treacle	1 teaspoon molasses

Melt the butter and oil together and fry the onion and apple for 2 minutes. Add the curry powder and the flour and cook gently for 2 minutes. Add the salt and pepper, bay leaf, garlic and stock and cook gently for 1 hour. Add the chutney, lemon juice and treacle. Leave to stand for several hours before using as this improves the flavour immensely.
Cooking time 1 hour 5 minutes

Vegetables

Here are a few ideas to liven up everyday vegetables: Chopped fresh parsley and a knob of butter make a great difference to almost all plain boiled vegetables; try a teaspoonful of mint sauce stirred into peas; and some nutmeg sprinkled over Brussels sprouts.

Glazed carrots

Imperial/Metric	American
1 lb./450 g. carrots	1 lb. carrots
salt and pepper	salt and pepper
1 teaspoon sugar	1 teaspoon sugar
1 oz./25 g. butter	2 tablespoons butter
1 tablespoon chopped parsley	1 tablespoon chopped parsley

Cut the carrots into fairly thin strips. Put them in a saucepan with the salt and pepper, sugar and butter. Just cover with water and boil with the lid on until just tender. Remove the lid and boil fast until all the liquid evaporates and the carrots are left with a rich glaze on top. Watch them carefully for the last few minutes or they will burn. Add the chopped parsley and serve.
Cooking time 15–20 minutes

Baked cabbage

This is well worth the extra few minutes to prepare, as it bears no resemblance to that horrible soft wet mess usually referred to as 'plain boiled cabbage'.

Imperial/Metric	American
1 white cabbage	1 white cabbage
2 oz./50 g. butter	¼ cup butter
1 medium-sized onion	1 medium-sized onion
bay leaf and pinch mixed herbs	bay leaf and pinch mixed herbs
salt and freshly ground black pepper	salt and freshly ground black pepper

Cut the cabbage in half, remove the stalk, cut the cabbage into fairly thin slices. Put into a saucepan of boiling water for 2 minutes and drain. Butter an ovenproof dish, put the cabbage into the dish. Slice the onion and put this on top of the cabbage together with the bay leaf, pinch of mixed herbs, remaining butter and salt and pepper. Cook in a moderate oven until the cabbage is still slightly nutty, should be about 20 minutes, but it does depend on the age and quality of the cabbage.
Cooking time about 20 minutes
Oven temperature 350°F., 180°C., Gas Mark 4

Scalloped potatoes

This is one of the few ways of preparing potatoes that requires no last-minute attention.

Imperial/Metric	American
potatoes (see method)	potatoes (see method)
butter	butter
salt and pepper	salt and pepper
milk or stock	milk or stock
onions (optional)	onions (optional)
grated cheese (optional)	grated cheese (optional)

Peel and thinly slice the required quantity of potatoes. Butter a suitable fairly shallow ovenproof dish and put the potatoes with a generous sprinkling of salt and pepper in layers in the dish. Pour in enough milk almost to cover the potatoes and put a few dots of butter on the top. Cook uncovered in a moderate oven for approximately 50–60 minutes. Vary this by putting a few layers of sliced onion in the dish, or if you think it might be too rich, pour stock over the potatoes instead of milk. We like the onion version with a little grated cheese on top of each onion layer and plenty of grated cheese on the top. Do not leave the sliced potatoes in water before using as this takes away some of the starch, making the dish far less creamy.
Cooking time 50–60 minutes
Oven temperature 350°F., 180°C., Gas Mark 4

Corn fritters

Very good with cold ham, fried chicken or salad.

Imperial/Metric	American
2 eggs	2 eggs
2 tablespoons milk	3 tablespoons milk
2 tablespoons flour	3 tablespoons flour
½ teaspoon salt	½ teaspoon salt
1 16-oz./454-g. can creamed corn	1 16-oz. can creamed corn
oil	oil

Separate the eggs; beat the yolks until thick and light. Mix together the milk, flour and salt, then combine with the egg yolks and corn. (If you have trouble finding creamed corn put a can of ordinary corn in the blender for a few seconds.) Whip the egg whites until stiff but not dry. Gently fold in the corn mixture. Heat a little oil in a heavy frying pan and cook by dropping tablespoonfuls of the mixture into the hot pan. When the underside is golden brown, turn and gently cook the other side. Drain and serve very hot.
Cooking time few minutes

Courgettes or marrow with tomatoes

Imperial/Metric	American
1 tablespoon corn oil	1 tablespoon corn oil
1 oz./25 g. butter	2 tablespoons butter
1 large onion, chopped	1 large onion, chopped
1 lb./450 g. courgettes or marrow	1 lb. zucchini
1 15-oz./425-g. can tomatoes	1 15-oz. can tomatoes
1 clove garlic, crushed	1 clove garlic, crushed
pinch mixed herbs	pinch mixed herbs
salt and pepper	salt and pepper

Heat the oil and butter in a pan and fry the onion until golden. Spread the onion on the bottom of a lidded casserole dish, cut the courgettes or marrow in rounds and put on top of the onions. Pour the tomatoes over and add the garlic, herbs and seasoning. Cover and cook in a moderate oven for about 40 minutes, until the courgettes are tender. Serve with pork.
Cooking time about 40 minutes
Oven temperature 350°F., 180°C., Gas Mark 4

Sweetcorn with almonds

Imperial/Metric	American
2 oz./50 g. blanched almonds, flaked	½ cup blanched almonds, flaked
3 oz./75 g. butter	6 tablespoons butter
1 can sweetcorn	1 can corn
salt and pepper	salt and pepper

Fry the almonds slowly in butter until they are a pale gold. Add the drained sweetcorn and heat through gently. Season to taste.
Cooking time few minutes

French beans with lemon juice

Imperial/Metric	American
2 oz./50 g. butter	¼ cup butter
1 lb./450 g. small French beans	1 lb. small green beans
juice of 1 lemon	juice of 1 lemon
salt and pepper	salt and pepper

Melt the butter in a lidded frying pan, add the beans, lemon juice and seasoning and cover tightly. Cook for 10 minutes, shaking the pan often so that the beans are well covered with the lemon glaze. Do not add any water. The beans should be just slightly crisp when ready, not soggy.
Cooking time 10 minutes

Reiko's onion fritters

These are delicious with cold meat, bacon or cheese.

Imperial/Metric	American
4 oz./100 g. plain flour	1 cup all-purpose flour
½ teaspoon salt	½ teaspoon salt
1 lb./450 g. onions	1 lb. onions
oil	oil

Mix the flour and salt with enough cold water to make a thick batter. Peel and thickly slice the onions, dip in batter and fry in ¼-inch (½-cm.) deep oil until golden and tender. Drain well.
Cooking time few minutes

Puddings

Swiss breakfast cereal

Children love making this, and it's much cheaper than the bought variety. Serve it for breakfast, supper, or even as a pudding.

Imperial/Metric	American
1 lb./450 g. rolled oats	4½ cups rolled oats
6 Weetabix, crushed	1½ cups Wheaties
5 oz./150 g. mixed raisins and sultanas	1 cup mixed dark and white raisins
2 oz./50 g. walnuts or hazelnuts, chopped	½ cup chopped walnuts or hazelnuts
2 oz./50 g. flaked almonds	½ cup flaked almonds

Mix all the ingredients together and stir well. Keep in an airtight plastic box or a tin, and serve with brown sugar and milk to taste.

Apple and sultana snow

Imperial/Metric	American
2 lb./900 g. cooking apples	2 lb. cooking apples
2 tablespoons water	3 tablespoons water
2–4 oz./50–100 g. sugar	¼–½ cup sugar
3 oz./75 g. sultanas	½ cup white raisins
grated rind of ½ orange and ½ lemon	grated rind of ½ orange and ½ lemon
2 eggs	2 eggs

Peel and slice the apples and cook with the water until soft. Add sugar to taste and stir until it dissolves. Cool. Put into the blender with the sultanas, orange and lemon rind and egg yolks. Blend until smooth. Beat the egg whites until stiff and fold the apple mixture into them. Chill well.
Cooking time few minutes

Lamb chops in casserole (page 13), stuffed frankfurters (page 17) and beef Louisiana (page 12)

Apricot condé

Imperial/Metric
1 lemon jelly

¾ pint/4 dl. boiling
  water
1 15½-oz./439-g. can
  apricot halves
1 15½-oz./439-g. can
  rice pudding

American
1 package lemon-
  flavored gelatin
1½ cups boiling water

1 14-oz. can apricot
  halves
1 14-oz. can rice
  pudding

Make up the jelly with the boiling water and leave
to cool. Drain the apricots, reserve four and chop
the remainder. Add the juice to the jelly. Put the
chopped apricots and rice in a bowl, stir in ¾ pint
(4 dl., 1½ cups) of the cooled jelly, mix well and pour
into four glasses. Leave in a cool place until just set.
Put an apricot half on the top of each glass and spoon
over the remaining jelly. This also works well with
pineapple, mandarin oranges and strawberries.
Illustrated on page 23

Danish apricot pudding

This is particularly good in the winter when there
are very few fresh fruits available and everyone is
getting fed up with apple puddings and canned fruit.

Imperial/Metric
8 oz./225 g. dried
  apricots
2 oz./50 g. sugar, or
  to taste
1 pint/6 dl. water
2 teaspoons lemon
  juice
3 oz./75 g. butter
1 tablespoon soft
  brown sugar
6 oz./175 g. white
  breadcrumbs,
  preferably made
  with slightly stale
  bread
¼ pint/1½ dl. double
  cream
1 bar flaky chocolate,
  plain

American
1½ cups dried apricots

¼ cup sugar, or to
  taste
2½ cups water
2 teaspoons lemon
  juice
6 tablespoons butter
1 tablespoon soft
  brown sugar
2 cups white bread
  crumbs, preferably
  made with slightly
  stale bread

⅔ cup whipping cream

1 bar semi-sweet
  chocolate

Put the apricots, sugar and water in a saucepan and
bring to the boil; cover and simmer for 40 minutes or
until tender. Liquidise the fruit with the syrup, or
sieve to make a purée. Stir in the lemon juice and
leave to get cold. Melt the butter, mix the brown
sugar and the breadcrumbs together and fry until

golden brown. Put a third of the crumb mixture into
a glass dish, cover with half the apricot mixture,
cover this with another third of the crumbs, cover
this with the last of the fruit and top with the crumbs.
Leave for a few hours in the refrigerator or overnight if you can manage it. Whip the cream and use
to decorate the pudding. Crumble the chocolate and
sprinkle over the cream.
Cooking time about 40 minutes

Quick butterscotch ice cream

Imperial/Metric
1 packet
  butterscotch
  instant whip
½ pint/3 dl. milk
1 small can
  evaporated milk
1 tablespoon instant
  coffee
about 2 oz./50 g.
  chopped walnuts
  (optional)

American
1 package
  butterscotch
  instant whip
1¼ cups milk
1 small can
  evaporated milk
1 tablespoon instant
  coffee
about ½ cup chopped
  walnuts (optional)

Make up the instant whip with the milk and the
evaporated milk and beat well. Stir in the coffee
mixed with a little water; add the nuts and freeze
until firm, about 3 hours. Take the ice cream out of
the freezer about 15 minutes before serving, otherwise it's like a rock! Older children can make this
themselves.
Freezing time about 3 hours

Fruit fools

Imperial/Metric
½ pint/3 dl. thick
  custard
1 lb./450 g. cooked
  fruit, apples,
  gooseberries,
  apricots, rhubarb,
  etc.
little cream

American
1¼ cups thick custard

1 lb. cooked fruit,
  apples,
  gooseberries,
  apricots, rhubarb,
  etc.
little cream

Make up the custard as instructed on the packet or
tin or make homemade custard. Leave to cool a little.
Cool the fruit, then blend and sieve. Mix the purée
with the custard and blend together for a few seconds,
a little at a time. Taste for sweetness. Stir in a little
cream if you have some. Leave to set and decorate
with cream and glacé cherries if liked. For a much
richer fool the custard can be replaced by whipped
cream simply folded into the purée.

Biscuit base fruit flan

Imperial/Metric	American
base	base
6 oz./175 g. biscuit crumbs, digestive, Marie or ginger	1½ cups cookie crumbs, graham cracker or ginger snap
3 oz./75 g. margarine	6 tablespoons margarine
1½ oz./40 g. castor sugar	3 tablespoons granulated sugar
filling	filling
1 lb./450 g. fresh fruit purée, apples, pears or apricots, or 1 can fruit pie filling	2 cups fresh fruit purée, apples, pears or apricots, or 1 can fruit pie filling
meringue top	meringue top
2 egg whites	2 egg whites
4 oz./100 g. castor sugar	½ cup granulated sugar

To make the base, crush the biscuits with a rolling pin or milk bottle to make fine crumbs. Melt the margarine and sugar together in a saucepan and add to the crumbs. Mix well and press over the base and sides of an 8-inch (20-cm.) flan dish. Put in the fridge until cold. Spread the fruit purée over the biscuit base.

To make the meringue, beat the egg whites until stiff and add the sugar and beat again. Spread evenly over the fruit purée and put into a moderately hot oven for 5 minutes or until lightly brown. Cool.

Cooking time 5 minutes

Oven temperature 400°F., 200°C., Gas Mark 6

Variations

This biscuit base could be used for lemon meringue pie. The ginger biscuit base is especially good with pears.

Frozen lemon crunch

Imperial/Metric	American
1 oz./25 g. butter	2 tablespoons butter
5 tablespoons castor sugar	6 tablespoons granulated sugar
2 oz./50 g. cornflake crumbs	1 cup cornflake crumbs
2 eggs, separated	2 eggs, separated
1 small can condensed milk	1 small can condensed milk
4 tablespoons lemon juice	⅓ cup lemon juice

Melt the butter and stir in 2 tablespoons of the sugar and the cornflake crumbs. Put this mixture into an ice cube tray and press down and around the sides. Beat the egg yolks until thick and creamy, then slowly add the condensed milk and lemon juice, beating all the time. Beat the egg whites until stiff, then slowly add the remaining sugar. Fold together, using a metal spoon. Spoon into the tray and put into the ice compartment several hours before eating.

Freezing time about 3 hours

Illustrated on page 51

Coffee fudge pie

Imperial/Metric	American
7 oz./200 g. shortcrust pastry	basic pie dough made with 1¾ cups flour
2 tablespoons apricot jam	3 tablespoons apricot jam
3 oz./75 g. margarine	6 tablespoons margarine
3 oz./75 g. castor sugar	6 tablespoons granulated sugar
1 egg	1 egg
2 oz./50 g. walnuts, finely chopped	½ cup finely chopped walnuts
4 oz./100 g. self-raising flour	1 cup all-purpose flour sifted with 1 teaspoon baking powder
1 tablespoon liquid coffee essence	1 tablespoon liquid coffee flavoring
2 teaspoons milk	2 teaspoons milk
¼ pint/1½ dl. sour cream	⅔ cup sour cream

Line a 9-inch (23-cm.) flan case with the pastry and spread the apricot jam on the bottom. Cream the margarine and sugar together until fluffy and beat in the egg and walnuts. Fold in the flour with the coffee essence and milk. Pour into the pastry case. Smooth the top and bake in a moderately hot oven for 15 minutes. Lower the heat to moderate and cook for a further 15–20 minutes. Stick a cocktail stick into the centre and if it comes out clean the pie is done. Remove from the oven and cover with the sour cream. Put back for 2 minutes. Serve hot.

Cooking time 30–35 minutes

Oven temperature 400°F., 200°C., Gas Mark 6, then 350°F., 180°C., Gas Mark 4

Illustrated on page 31

Apple and mincemeat flan

Imperial/Metric	American
6 oz./175 g. shortcrust pastry	basic pie dough made with 1½ cups flour
6 tablespoons mincemeat	½ cup mincemeat
2 large cooking apples	2 large cooking apples
juice of ½ lemon	juice of ½ lemon
2 tablespoons castor sugar	2 tablespoons granulated sugar

Line an 8-inch (20-cm.) flan tin with pastry and spread the mincemeat over the base. Peel and quarter the apples and cut into thin slices. Lay these over the mincemeat carefully in a spiral starting from the centre. Pour lemon juice over and sprinkle with 1 tablespoon castor sugar. Bake in a moderately hot oven for 35–40 minutes. If the pastry gets too brown, lower the heat after 20 minutes. Remove and sprinkle with remaining sugar. Serve hot or cold.

Cooking time 35–40 minutes
Oven temperature 375°F., 190°C., Gas Mark 5
Illustrated opposite

Variations
You can use apple purée instead of the slices if you like, and if you add a pastry lid this makes a very good pie.

For a change, use red-skinned eating apples and do not peel them. Lay the slices overlapping round the edge of the flan as in the picture opposite.

Yogurt in a vacuum flask

This simple method of making yogurt is useful if you eat a lot of it, as it's very cheap compared to the bought kind and can be flavoured with anything you like. We like it best with soft light brown sugar.

Imperial/Metric	American
1½ pints/scant litre milk	4 cups milk
2 tablespoons dried milk	3 tablespoons dried milk
1 tablespoon plain yogurt	1 tablespoon plain yogurt

Put the milk and the dried milk into a saucepan and heat to 180°F. (82°C.), using a sugar thermometer for accuracy. Cool to 120°F. (49°C.). Add the plain yogurt and stir well. Pour into a large vacuum flask and close the lid tightly. Leave overnight, and in the morning shake out the yogurt into a bowl and put into the fridge to go cold. A tablespoon of this can be used as the starter for subsequent batches.

Sauces for ice cream
Butterscotch sauce

Imperial/Metric	American
4 oz./100 g. soft brown sugar	½ cup soft brown sugar
2 tablespoons plain flour	3 tablespoons all-purpose flour
pinch salt	pinch salt
9 tablespoons/2 dl. boiling water	⅔ cup boiling water
1 oz./25 g. butter	2 tablespoons butter
few drops vanilla essence	few drops vanilla extract
3 tablespoons cream	¼ cup coffee cream

In a small saucepan mix together the sugar, flour and salt. Slowly pour in the boiling water, stirring well. Heat gently, stirring constantly until the mixture thickens, beat well, remove from heat. Stir in the butter, vanilla and cream. Best hot or warm.

Chocolate nut sauce

Imperial/Metric	American
5 oz./150 g. chocolate chips	1 cup chocolate chips
2 tablespoons soft brown sugar	3 tablespoons soft brown sugar
2 tablespoons water	3 tablespoons water
½ oz./15 g. butter	1 tablespoon butter
few chopped walnuts	few chopped walnuts

Put the chocolate in a small saucepan with the sugar and water and heat very gently, stirring well until smooth. Cut the butter in small pieces and stir in slowly; add the nuts and serve the sauce hot.

Coffee raisin sauce

Imperial/Metric	American
4 tablespoons golden syrup	⅓ cup maple syrup
2 oz./50 g. raisins	⅓ cup raisins
¼ pint/1½ dl. water	⅔ cup water
1 tablespoon cornflour	1 tablespoon cornstarch
1 tablespoon instant coffee	1 tablespoon instant coffee

Put the syrup, raisins and water in a small saucepan, bring to the boil, reduce the heat and simmer. Mix the cornflour and coffee in a small bowl with 1 tablespoon water. Add to the pan and bring to the boil again. Cool; keep in the fridge until required.

Coffee fudge pie (page 29) and apple and mincemeat flan

Two-way stretch

Time, to a mother with small children, is always in short supply, especially between five and seven in the evening. When you come back to the kitchen having finally persuaded your children to go to bed – and to stay there – the last thing you want to do is start preparing a meal from scratch. These recipes will help you avoid this by concentrating preparation time in the morning.

With a little cunning, the same ingredients can end up both in the children's lunch and in your supper. The size of your family will control the proportions in which you divide up your 'foundation' material, but the principle will remain the same.

Suppertime will become more relaxed and need no longer be the frantic climax to your evening rush-hour. When your husband comes home in the evening, he doesn't want to find you up to your elbows in potato peelings, and would much rather you had time to sit with him, with all or most of the cooking already out of the way.

Lunch Macaroni cheese

Prepare the supper in the morning and keep in the fridge.

Imperial/Metric	American
6 oz./175 g. cut macaroni	1½ cups cut macaroni
2 pints/generous litre salted water	5 cups salted water
1 oz./25 g. margarine	2 tablespoons margarine
1 oz./25 g. flour	¼ cup flour
¾ pint/4 dl. milk	scant 2 cups milk
1 teaspoon made English mustard	1 teaspoon made English mustard
4 oz./100 g. Cheddar cheese, grated	1 cup grated Cheddar cheese
salt and pepper	salt and pepper
Parmesan cheese	Parmesan cheese

Cook the macaroni in the water for about 15 minutes until tender and drain well. Meanwhile make a white sauce with the margarine, flour and milk and add the mustard and cheese. Season to taste. Add the macaroni to the sauce and mix well. Divide in half; put the lunchtime macaroni into a pie dish, sprinkle with the Parmesan cheese and brown under the grill or in the oven.

Cooking time about 25 minutes

Supper Italian macaroni cheese

Imperial/Metric	American
1 3½-oz./99-g. can tuna fish, drained	1 3½-oz. can tuna fish, drained
remaining macaroni in sauce	remaining macaroni in sauce
3 anchovy fillets	3 anchovy fillets
9 black olives	9 ripe olives
1–2 tomatoes, sliced	1–2 tomatoes, sliced
Parmesan cheese	Parmesan cheese

Flake the tuna fish, add to the macaroni and put into a pie dish. Cut the anchovy fillets in half lengthways and lay in a criss-cross pattern on top of the dish. Dot with black olives and tomato slices and sprinkle some Parmesan cheese on the top. Cover with a piece of foil and reheat gently in a moderate oven for 15 minutes, then remove the foil and cook for a further 15 minutes until brown on top.

Cooking time 30 minutes

Oven temperature 325°F., 160°C., Gas Mark 3

Lunch **Fish in cheese sauce**

Imperial/Metric	American
1½ lb./675 g. white fish, cod or coley	1½ lb. white fish, cod or haddock
¾ pint/4 dl. milk	2 cups milk
bay leaf	bay leaf
salt and pepper	salt and pepper
1 oz./25 g. margarine or butter	2 tablespoons margarine or butter
1 oz./25 g. flour	¼ cup flour
2–3 oz./50–75 g. cheese, grated	½–¾ cup grated cheese
chopped parsley	chopped parsley

Wash the fish and cut it into manageable pieces, about 5 inches (13 cm.) long. Put the fish into a saucepan and cover with the milk. Add the bay leaf and season with salt and pepper. Bring gently to the boil and simmer for 5 minutes. Remove the fish and flake it, taking out all the bones and pieces of skin. Divide the fish in half, keeping half on one side for supper. Meanwhile, melt the margarine in a small saucepan and add the flour and the fish milk to make a white sauce. Season well and cook for 3 minutes. Add the grated cheese and stir until it has melted. Fold in the fish and reheat gently. Add some chopped parsley, and serve with mashed potatoes and carrots for lunch.

Cooking time 10–15 minutes

Supper **Fish fritters**

Imperial/Metric	American
remaining flaked fish	remaining flaked fish
2 tablespoons finely chopped capers	3 tablespoons finely chopped capers
deep fat or oil for frying	deep fat or oil for frying
1 oz./25 g. cheese, finely grated (optional)	¼ cup finely grated cheese (optional)
fritter batter	fritter batter
4 oz./100 g. plain flour	1 cup all-purpose flour
½ teaspoon salt	½ teaspoon salt
little pepper	little pepper
¼ pint/1½ dl. lukewarm water	⅔ cup lukewarm water
1 tablespoon melted butter	1 tablespoon melted butter
2 egg whites, beaten	2 egg whites, beaten

First make the fritter batter by putting the flour, salt and pepper into a bowl and gradually mixing with the water and butter to make a thick, smooth batter. Whisk the egg whites until stiff, but do not add yet.

Mix the fish and capers into the batter mixture, and then fold in the egg whites. Drop spoonfuls into hot oil and fry till well puffed up and golden, about 2–3 minutes. Drain on kitchen paper and if you like, sprinkle with cheese. Serve with tartare sauce, the bought variety in this case.

Cooking time 2–3 minutes

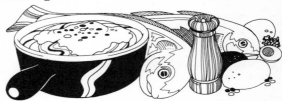

Lunch **Fish pie**

You can prepare the supper at lunchtime and just reheat it in the evening.

Imperial/Metric	American
1 lb./450 g. white fish, cod or coley	1 lb. white fish, cod or haddock
¼ pint/1½ dl. water	⅔ cup water
½ pint/3 dl. milk	1¼ cups milk
bay leaf	bay leaf
salt and pepper	salt and pepper
1½ oz./40 g. margarine	3 tablespoons margarine
1 oz./25 g. flour	¼ cup flour
1 tablespoon chopped parsley	1 tablespoon chopped parsley
2 hard-boiled eggs, chopped	2 hard-cooked eggs, chopped
2 lb./900 g. mashed potatoes	4 cups mashed potatoes
tomatoes (optional)	tomatoes (optional)

Simmer the fish in the water and milk with the bay leaf and salt and pepper. Drain, retaining the fish liquor for the sauce. Flake the fish. Make a white sauce with the margarine, flour and fish liquor and add the parsley. Season again if necessary. Add the fish and the hard-boiled eggs, chopped small. Now divide the fish mixture in half. Put one half into a pie dish and top with half the mashed potatoes. Cook in a moderately hot oven for 30 minutes until brown and bubbly. Garnish with sliced tomatoes if your children like them.

Cooking time 40 minutes
Oven temperature 375°F., 190°C., Gas Mark 5
Illustrated on page 55

Supper Scalloped fish

If you ask your fishmonger he will probably give you the scallop shells for nothing – at least ours did!

Imperial/Metric	American
2 oz./50 g. cheese, grated	½ cup grated cheese
1 teaspoon capers	1 teaspoon capers
1 small can shrimps (optional)	1 small can shrimp (optional)
remaining fish mixture	remaining fish mixture
4 scallop shells, buttered	4 scallop shells, buttered
remaining mashed potatoes	remaining mashed potatoes
extra cheese (optional)	extra cheese (optional)

Add the cheese, capers and shrimps, if using them, to the fish mixture and put a spoonful in the middle of each of the scallop shells. Pipe or spoon the mashed potatoes round the edge and sprinkle with a little more cheese if you like. Cook in a moderately hot oven for 20 minutes until the potato is well browned.

Cooking time 20 minutes
Oven temperature 400°F., 200°C., Gas Mark 6
Illustrated on page 55

Lunch Mince with baked beans

Imperial/Metric	American
1 tablespoon oil	1 tablespoon oil
1 lb./450 g. minced beef	1 lb. ground beef
2 onions, chopped	2 onions, chopped
1 small can tomatoes	1 small can tomatoes
pinch herbs	pinch herbs
garlic salt	garlic salt
black pepper	black pepper
1 large can baked beans	1 large can baked beans

Heat the oil in a large lidded frying pan or saucepan. Fry the meat and the onions for 5 minutes. Add the tomatoes and herbs and season to taste. Bring to the boil and simmer for 20 minutes until the meat is tender. Add the baked beans and heat through gently.

Take out enough for the children's lunch and serve with mashed potatoes and a green vegetable.

Cooking time 25 minutes

Supper Chilli con carne

Imperial/Metric	American
remaining mince and beans	remaining ground beef and beans
½ green pepper, blanched (optional)	½ green sweet pepper, blanched (optional)
chilli powder to taste (or cayenne pepper)	chili powder to taste (or cayenne pepper)
1 small can baked beans	1 small can baked beans

Reheat the mince mixture with the chopped green pepper and add the chilli powder and the extra baked beans. Go carefully if you are using cayenne pepper as it is very hot. Mix well together and simmer very gently for 5 minutes. Serve with a fresh tomato salad.

Cooking time 5 minutes

Lunch Hamburgers

It is worth while asking the butcher to mince you a piece of chuck steak or mincing it yourself for this recipe, as butcher's mince is so fatty. However, it is not vital.

Imperial/Metric	American
2 slices bread	2 slices bread
little milk	little milk
1 medium-sized onion	1 medium-sized onion
1 egg	1 egg
1 lb./450 g. minced beef	1 lb. ground beef
salt and pepper	salt and pepper
little oil	little oil
cheese (optional)	cheese (optional)

Break the bread into pieces and soak in a little milk. Grate or finely mince the onion; if you have a blender put it in with the egg to pulp it. Mix the meat with the bread, egg and onion and season. Divide the mixture. Shape the children's portion into hamburgers and fry in a little oil. For a pleasant change try a slice of cheese put on to each hamburger after it is cooked and placed under the grill for just long enough to melt the cheese.

Cooking time few minutes

Supper **Meatballs in hot pepper sauce**

Imperial/Metric	American
remaining meat mixture	**remaining meat mixture**
little flour	**little flour**
little oil	**little oil**
sauce	sauce
1 onion	**1 onion**
1 small or ½ large green pepper	**1 small or ½ large green sweet pepper**
1 tablespoon flour	**1 tablespoon flour**
1 small can tomatoes	**1 small can tomatoes**
bay leaf	**bay leaf**
salt and pepper	**salt and pepper**
garlic salt	**garlic salt**
pinch sugar	**pinch sugar**
Worcestershire sauce and cayenne pepper to taste	**Worcestershire sauce and cayenne pepper to taste**

Shape the rest of the meat mixture into balls; flour and fry lightly in a little oil. Drain on kitchen paper.

To make the sauce, chop the onion and green pepper. Fry the onion in the pan you used for the meatballs, adding a little more oil if necessary; when soft add the green pepper. Fry for a few minutes, then stir in the flour followed by the rest of the ingredients. Transfer to a saucepan or casserole and add the meatballs. Leave all this until the evening then simmer the meatballs in the sauce for at least 30 minutes. Serve with pasta and a salad.
Cooking time about 35 minutes

Lunch **Cottage pie**

Imperial/Metric	American
1½ lb./675 g. finely minced beef	**1½ lb. finely ground beef**
2 large onions, chopped	**2 large onions, chopped**
pinch mixed herbs	**pinch mixed herbs**
1 tablespoon tomato purée	**1 tablespoon tomato paste**
salt and pepper	**salt and pepper**
pinch garlic salt	**pinch garlic salt**
1 tablespoon flour	**1 tablespoon flour**
¾ pint/4 dl. beef stock	**2 cups beef stock**
1 tablespoon Worcestershire sauce	**1 tablespoon Worcestershire sauce**
3 carrots, diced	**3 carrots, diced**
1 lb./450 g. mashed potatoes	**2 cups mashed potatoes**

Fry the mince quickly until the fat begins to run and it goes brown. Add the onions and fry gently for 5 minutes. Add the herbs, tomato purée, salt, pepper and garlic salt and stir well. Stir in the flour and cook for 1 minute before adding the stock and Worcestershire sauce. At this stage divide the mixture in half. Add the diced carrots to one and cook gently with a lid on for 30 minutes. Transfer to an ovenproof dish, top with the mashed potatoes and put into the oven to brown. Serve hot with a green vegetable.
Cooking time about 45 minutes
Oven temperature 375°F., 190°C., Gas Mark 5

Supper **Spaghetti bolognese**

Imperial/Metric	American
remaining mince mixture	**remaining ground beef mixture**
2 tablespoons tomato purée	**3 tablespoons tomato paste**
1 clove garlic, crushed	**1 clove garlic, crushed**
pinch thyme and oregano	**pinch thyme and oregano**
½ teaspoon sugar	**½ teaspoon sugar**
¼ pint/1½ dl. beef stock	**⅔ cup beef stock**
4–6 oz./100–150 g. spaghetti	**4–6 oz. spaghetti**
2 oz./50 g. cheese, grated	**½ cup grated cheese**

Heat up the remaining mince mixture and add the purée, garlic, herbs, sugar and stock and cook gently for 30 minutes. Serve on top of spaghetti cooked in the usual way, and sprinkle with cheese.
Cooking time 30 minutes

Lunch Simple lamb or veal stew

Imperial/Metric	American
1 lb./450 g. stewing veal or lamb cut from a small half shoulder	1 lb. stewing veal or lamb cut from the shoulder
1½ pints/1 litre cold water	4 cups cold water
salt and pepper	salt and pepper
little thyme	little thyme
2 medium-sized onions	2 medium-sized onions
8 oz./225 g. carrots	3–4 carrots
2 stalks celery	2 stalks celery
potatoes	potatoes
1 tablespoon tomato purée (optional)	1 tablespoon tomato paste (optional)

Cut the meat into small pieces, put into a large saucepan with the water and bring to the boil. Remove the scum, add salt, pepper and thyme, simmer for 30 minutes. Peel and slice the onions and carrots, wash and slice the celery, add the vegetables and cook for another ¾–1 hour or until the meat is tender. Strain the liquid into a large jug. Take out the amount of meat and vegetables needed for the children. Dice their potatoes and cook until tender in a little of the meat stock; add their meat and vegetables with a little more stock, stir in the tomato purée and heat thoroughly.
Cooking time 1½–2 hours

Supper Lamb or veal with Greek lemon sauce

Imperial/Metric	American
remaining stew	remaining stew
sauce	sauce
2 egg yolks	2 egg yolks
2 tablespoons lemon juice	2½ tablespoons lemon juice
1 oz./25 g. butter	2 tablespoons butter
1 oz./25 g. flour	¼ cup flour
½ pint/3 dl. stock	1¼ cups stock
salt and pepper	salt and pepper
little chopped parsley	little chopped parsley

Heat the stew with a very little liquid. Mix the two yolks with the lemon juice (if you separate the eggs in the morning you can use the whites for meringues and have a pudding for everyone). In a small saucepan melt the butter, stir in the flour and cook for 1 minute; slowly stir in the stock and bring to the boil, stirring constantly. Simmer for a few minutes, then mix a few spoonfuls of this sauce with the eggs and lemon juice, return to the pan and season. Put the meat in a serving dish and pour over the sauce, sprinkle with parsley and serve with rice.
Cooking time few minutes

Lunch Roast lamb with herbs

Imperial/Metric	American
2 lb./900 g. best end of neck, in one piece	2 lb. rolled shoulder of lamb
1 clove garlic	1 clove garlic
1 teaspoon thyme and rosemary	1 teaspoon thyme and rosemary
bay leaf, crushed	bay leaf, crushed
salt and pepper	salt and pepper
1 teaspoon grated lemon rind (optional)	1 teaspoon grated lemon rind (optional)
1 tablespoon oil	1 tablespoon oil

Ask the butcher to bone the lamb for you. Open the joint out and rub with the garlic. Mix the thyme, rosemary and bay leaf together and sprinkle over the inside surface of the meat. Season well and sprinkle the lemon rind over if using it. Roll up the joint neatly and tie with string in several places. Rub all over with the oil and cook in a moderate oven for 30 minutes per lb. (½ kg.). Baste with the pan juices. Serve with roast potatoes and salad.
Cooking time 30 minutes per lb. (½ kg.)
Oven temperature 350°F., 180°C., Gas Mark 4

Supper Cold lamb and hot potato salad or curry

Imperial/Metric	American
cold lamb	cold lamb
hot potato salad	hot potato salad
potatoes	potatoes
1 onion, finely chopped	1 onion, finely chopped
1 teaspoon French mustard	1 teaspoon French mustard
French dressing	French dressing
or	or
curry sauce (see page 24)	curry sauce (see page 24)

Either serve the lamb cold cut into neat, thin slices, with a hot potato salad, or cut into chunks, cover with curry sauce (see page 24) and serve with rice. To make the hot potato salad, cook some potatoes until only just tender and cut them into chunks. Add the finely chopped onion and the French mustard to the French dressing. Stir well and pour over the hot potatoes.

Lunch **Toad in the hole popovers**

Imperial/Metric	American
1 lb./450 g. chipolata sausages	**1 lb. small sausage links**
1 tablespoon oil	**1 tablespoon oil**
2 oz./50 g. plain flour	**½ cup all-purpose flour**
1 egg	**1 egg**
salt and pepper	**salt and pepper**
½ pint/3 dl. milk	**1¼ cups milk**
1 tablespoon oil or dripping	**1 tablespoon oil or drippings**

Fry half the sausages in the oil for 5 minutes or until brown all over. Put the flour into a mixing bowl and make a well in the middle. Into this put the egg and the salt and pepper. Beat gently for a moment and slowly add enough milk to form a smooth batter. Beat well for 2 minutes in case there are any lumps. Put a little oil or dripping into the bottom of six small patty tins and heat in a hot oven for 5 minutes. The oil must really be smoking hot to make the batter rise well. Cut each of the sausages into three, put three pieces into each of the hot patty tins and pour the batter over. Cook in a hot oven for about 15 minutes or until well risen and golden brown.
Cooking time about 25 minutes
Oven temperature 425°F., 220°C., Gas Mark 7

Supper **Sausage and bean bake**

This can be prepared for the oven in the morning.

Imperial/Metric	American
1 large onion, chopped	**1 large onion, chopped**
1 oz./25 g. butter	**2 tablespoons butter**
remaining sausages	**remaining sausages**
1 15-oz./425-g. can tomatoes	**1 15-oz. can tomatoes**
1 10-oz./283-g. can broad beans	**1 10-oz. can lima beans**
pinch mixed herbs	**pinch mixed herbs**
1 clove garlic, crushed (optional)	**1 clove garlic, crushed (optional)**
2 oz./50 g. white breadcrumbs and grated cheese, mixed	**¾ cup white bread crumbs and grated cheese, mixed**

Fry the onion and sausages in the butter for 5 minutes. Add the tomatoes and drained beans. Season to taste and add herbs and garlic if you like it. Cook in a moderate oven for 20 minutes with the lid on. Remove the lid, sprinkle the breadcrumbs and cheese over the top and continue cooking in a moderately hot oven for 10 minutes until brown and crisp.
Cooking time 35 minutes
Oven temperature 350°F., 180°C., Gas Mark 4, then 400°F., 200°C., Gas Mark 6

Lunch **Chicken in sauce**

Imperial/Metric	American
3 chicken joints	**3 chicken pieces**
1 carrot	**1 carrot**
1 onion	**1 onion**
bay leaf	**bay leaf**
salt and pepper	**salt and pepper**
½ pint/3 dl. white sauce	**1¼ cups white sauce**

Wash the chicken and place in a saucepan with the sliced carrot and onion; add the bay leaf and enough water to cover. Season. Simmer the chicken gently until tender. Remove the chicken from the stock and take the meat off the bone. Make the white sauce using a little of the stock and add the required quantity of chicken, the chopped carrot and onion. Season and serve with mashed potatoes and peas.
Cooking time about 30 minutes

Supper **Chicken pie**

Imperial/Metric	American
1½ oz./40 g. butter	**3 tablespoons butter**
1 oz./25 g. flour	**¼ cup flour**
½ pint/3 dl. milk or milk and stock	**1¼ cups milk or milk and stock**
1 small packet frozen mixed vegetables	**1 small package frozen mixed vegetables**
pinch nutmeg	**pinch nutmeg**
1 egg	**1 egg**
remaining chicken	**remaining chicken**
salt and pepper	**salt and pepper**
1 packet frozen puff pastry	**1 package frozen puff paste or pie crust mix**

Melt the butter, add the flour and slowly add the milk; bring to the boil and simmer for a few minutes. Stir in the frozen vegetables, nutmeg, the beaten egg and the chicken; season and stir well. Put this mixture in a pie dish. Roll out the pastry to cover the dish. Dampen the edges of the pie dish and cover with the pastry. Cook in a moderately hot oven for 30 minutes.
Cooking time 30 minutes
Oven temperature 400°F., 200°C., Gas Mark 6

Lunch **Liver and bacon nests**

Imperial/Metric	American
1 lb./450 g. potatoes	1 lb. potatoes
butter	butter
milk	milk
salt and pepper	salt and pepper
¾–1 lb./350–450 g. lamb's liver, sliced	¾–1 lb. lamb liver, sliced
seasoned flour	seasoned flour
oil	oil
2 rashers streaky bacon, chopped	2 slices bacon, chopped
1 onion, chopped	1 onion, chopped
½ teaspoon yeast extract (optional)	½ teaspoon gravy coloring (optional)

Cook the potatoes in salted water, drain, mash very well, mix with a good knob of butter, moisten with milk and season to taste. Cut the liver for the children in very small, thin pieces. Put the seasoned flour in a polythene bag and shake the liver in the flour. Heat a little oil and butter and fry the floured liver together with the bacon. Remove from the pan and fry the chopped onion. Then return the liver and bacon to the pan, sprinkle on a little seasoned flour, add the yeast extract if used, then add a little water; bring to the boil, stirring constantly. Make nests with part of the mashed potatoes on the children's plates, put the liver in the centre and serve with a green vegetable.

Cooking time about 20 minutes

Supper **Danish liver casserole**

This casserole can be prepared in the morning when cooking the children's lunch, then left to be cooked for supper in the evening.

Imperial/Metric	American
remaining liver	remaining liver
seasoned flour	seasoned flour
oil	oil
butter	butter
1 onion, chopped	1 onion, chopped
1 apple	1 apple
4 rashers streaky bacon	4 slices bacon
3 tablespoons milk or cream	¼ cup milk or cream
remaining mashed potatoes	remaining mashed potatoes

Shake the liver with the seasoned flour in a polythene bag. Fry the liver in a little oil and butter for 3 minutes on each side and remove to a casserole.

Fry the chopped onion until almost golden and put on top of the liver. Peel and chop the apple, fry for 1–2 minutes and put in the casserole. Remove the rinds from the bacon and put it on top of the apple. Pour the milk or cream over the casserole, spread the remaining mashed potato on top and mark with a fork. Cook in a moderate oven for 30 minutes, then brown under the grill if necessary. Spinach or beans go well with this dish.

Cooking time about 40 minutes
Oven temperature 350°F., 180°C., Gas Mark 4

Lunch **Roast chicken**

This may sound extravagant, but leftover chicken is so useful and can be made into curry, chicken salad or fricassee easily, as well as the recipe given below.

Imperial/Metric	American
1 3½- to 4-lb./1¼- to 1¾-kg. roasting chicken	1 3½- to 4-lb. chicken
2 oz./50 g. butter	¼ cup butter
4 pieces streaky bacon	4 slices bacon
salt and pepper	salt and pepper
little flour	little flour
giblet stock	giblet stock

Put the chicken into a roasting tin and cover with the butter. Lay the bacon over the breast to keep it moist during cooking and sprinkle with salt and pepper. Roast in a moderately hot oven for 1¼ hours, basting occasionally. Make some gravy with the pan juices, a little flour and stock made from the giblets.

Carve the breast for the children and keep the legs intact for the evening.

Cooking time 1¼ hours
Oven temperature 375°F., 190°C., Gas Mark 5

Supper **Chicken in mushroom sauce**

Imperial/Metric	American
2 chicken legs and chicken pieces from carcass	2 chicken legs and chicken pieces from carcass
1 oz./25 g. butter	2 tablespoons butter
4 oz./100 g. mushrooms, sliced	1 cup sliced mushrooms
1 can condensed mushroom soup	1 can condensed mushroom soup
gravy (optional)	gravy (optional)

Put the chicken into a casserole with a lid. Fry the mushrooms for a moment in the butter and lay them over the chicken. Cover with the soup and a little gravy from lunch if you made some, though this is not essential. Put in a moderate oven for 20–30 minutes. Serve with new potatoes.

Cooking time 20–30 minutes

Oven temperature 350°F., 180°C., Gas Mark 4

Lunch **Normandy casserole**

Imperial/Metric	American
1 lb./450 g. belly of pork, boned	1 lb. fresh pork picnic shoulder
2 tablespoons oil	3 tablespoons oil
2 small onions	2 small onions
3 carrots	3 carrots
1 leek	1 leek
3 stalks celery	3 stalks celery
4 oz./100 g. mushrooms	1 cup mushrooms
1 teaspoon flour	1 teaspoon flour
$\frac{1}{4}$ pint/1$\frac{1}{2}$ dl. chicken stock	$\frac{2}{3}$ cup chicken stock
salt and pepper	salt and pepper
dash Worcestershire sauce	dash Worcestershire sauce

Cut the meat into small pieces and remove as much fat as possible. Fry the meat in the oil for 5 minutes. Chop the onions, cut the carrots into strips, slice the leek and celery and quarter the mushrooms. Remove the meat, add the vegetables to the pan and fry slowly for 5–10 minutes. Now put half the meat and vegetables into a second casserole for supper. Add the flour to the remaining half, stir well, add the stock and bring to the boil. Season and add the Worcestershire sauce. Simmer for 30 minutes until the meat is tender and serve with potatoes.

Cooking time 40–45 minutes

Supper **Sweet and sour pork with pilaff**

Imperial/Metric	American
remaining pork and vegetables	remaining pork and vegetables
sweet and sour sauce	sweet and sour sauce
1 tablespoon cornflour	1 tablespoon cornstarch
2 teaspoons sugar	2 teaspoons sugar
$\frac{1}{4}$ pint/1$\frac{1}{2}$ dl. chicken stock	$\frac{2}{3}$ cup chicken stock
2 teaspoons tomato purée	2 teaspoons tomato paste
1 tablespoon vinegar, preferably wine	1 tablespoon vinegar, preferably wine
2 teaspoons soy sauce, or more to taste	2 teaspoons soy sauce, or more to taste
salt and pepper	salt and pepper
simple rice pilaff	simple rice pilaff
1$\frac{1}{2}$ oz./40 g. butter	3 tablespoons butter
1 small onion, chopped	1 small onion, chopped
8 oz./225 g. rice	1 cup rice
$\frac{3}{4}$ pint/4 dl. chicken stock made with 1 stock cube and water	2 cups chicken stock made with 1 bouillon cube and water
salt and pepper	salt and pepper
2 oz./50 g. sultanas	$\frac{1}{3}$ cup white raisins
1–2 oz./25–50 g. flaked almonds (optional)	$\frac{1}{4}$–$\frac{1}{2}$ cup flaked almonds (optional)

To make the sweet and sour sauce, put the cornflour and sugar into a bowl, slowly add the stock and stir well. Add the tomato purée, vinegar and soy sauce and pour into the casserole with the meat and vegetables. Season, bring to the boil and simmer for 25–30 minutes. Don't cook this for too long, as the vegetables are better very slightly crunchy.

Meanwhile, make the pilaff. Melt 1 oz. (25 g., 2 tablespoons) of the butter in a flameproof casserole, add the onion and cook slowly until golden. Stir in the rice and cook for 2–3 minutes. Pour in the stock, season and bring to the boil. Cover and cook in a moderately hot oven for 20 minutes, adding more stock if necessary. When cooked, add the rest of the butter with the sultanas and nuts and fork in carefully.

Cooking time 25–30 minutes

Oven temperature 375°F., 190°C., Gas Mark 5

Teatime

This is a meal which varies in every house and seems to change each year as the children grow up. We have only given recipes for tea breads, biscuits and cakes in this section plus a few rather special cakes, most of which would also be delicious as desserts. All the cake recipes are very simple; most of the sponge cakes rely on the all-in-together method, the secret to the success of these being the use of soft margarine and an electric mixer. Bought cakes and biscuits can easily run away with a large slice of your weekly grocery bill, and if you read the small print they often include rather dubious sounding ingredients. Somehow you don't begrudge the children another slice of cake when you know its ingredients include eggs. You will find several ideas for quickly cooked teas for older children in the quick suppers section (see page 58). We have made a note on the recipes which are simple enough for the children to help prepare without disaster.

Tea breads and scones

Banana bread

Imperial/Metric	American
1 egg	1 egg
5 oz./150 g. castor sugar	$\frac{2}{3}$ cup granulated sugar
1½ oz./40 g. butter, melted	3 tablespoons melted butter
3 ripe bananas	3 ripe bananas
8 oz./225 g. self-raising flour	2 cups all-purpose flour sifted with 2 teaspoons baking powder
¾ teaspoon bicarbonate of soda	¾ teaspoon baking soda
½ teaspoon salt	½ teaspoon salt

Beat the egg until light, add the sugar and melted butter, mix well and add the mashed bananas. Sift the dry ingredients and combine with the banana mixture. Pour the mixture into a greased 2-lb. (1-kg.) loaf tin and cook in a moderately hot oven for 50–60 minutes.

Cooking time 50–60 minutes
Oven temperature 375°F., 190°C., Gas Mark 5

Fruit bread

This is a marvellous recipe, so simple and always popular. It is delicious with butter but the children will eat it as cake. It also keeps very well.

Imperial/Metric	American
1 lb./450 g. mixed fruit	3 cups mixed dried fruit
½ pint/3 dl. cold tea	1¼ cups cold tea
10 oz./275 g. soft brown sugar	1¼ cups soft brown sugar
10 oz./275 g. self-raising flour	2½ cups all-purpose flour sifted with 2½ teaspoons baking powder
1 egg, beaten	1 egg, beaten

Leave the fruit to soak overnight with the tea and brown sugar. In the morning add the flour and beaten egg. Put in a buttered 2-lb. (1-kg.) loaf tin which has been lined with greased greaseproof paper, and cook in a moderate oven for 1½–2 hours. If the cake seems to be becoming too brown, cover with foil. Do not eat it until the day after it is made; it tastes so much better then.

Cooking time 1½–2 hours
Oven temperature 325°F., 160°C., Gas Mark 3

Date loaf

This recipe makes a 2-lb. (1-kg.) loaf or two 1-lb. (½-kg.) loaves.

Imperial/Metric	American
4 oz./100 g. plain flour	2 cups all-purpose
4 oz./100 g. self-raising flour	flour sifted with 1 teaspoon baking powder
8 oz./225 g. sugar	1 cup sugar
1 teaspoon bicarbonate of soda	1 teaspoon baking soda
1 oz./25 g. margarine	2 tablespoons margarine
1 egg, beaten	1 egg, beaten
6 oz./175 g. dates, covered with warm water	1 cup dates, covered with warm water

Sift the dry ingredients together in a bowl and rub in the margarine. Add the beaten egg and then the dates and their liquid. Mix to a soft dropping mixture, adding more water if necessary. Bake in a greased loaf tin in a moderate to moderately hot oven for about 1 hour. Stick a skewer into the centre, and if it comes out clean it's done. Cool in the tin for 10 minutes then turn out. Keep for a day before cutting if possible.

Cooking time about 1 hour
Oven temperature 350–375°F., 180–190°C., Gas Mark 4–5

Cheese and bacon loaf

Imperial/Metric	American
3 oz./75 g. soft margarine	6 tablespoons soft margarine
8 oz./225 g. self-raising flour	2 cups all-purpose flour
1 teaspoon baking powder	3 teaspoons baking powder
1 teaspoon dry mustard	1 teaspoon dry mustard
½ teaspoon salt	½ teaspoon salt
¼ teaspoon pepper	¼ teaspoon pepper
4 rashers bacon, chopped	4 slices bacon, chopped
1 egg	1 egg
3 oz./75 g. Cheddar cheese, grated	¾ cup grated Cheddar cheese
¼ pint/1½ dl. milk	⅔ cup milk

Put all the ingredients together in a large bowl and stir until they are well mixed together.

Grease a 1-lb. (½-kg.) loaf tin and put the mixture into it. Cook in a moderately hot oven for 45 minutes or until well risen and golden brown. Leave in the tin for a few minutes before turning out. Serve sliced and buttered when cold. This is also good for a light lunch with cheese, tomatoes and soup.

Cooking time 45 minutes
Oven temperature 375°F., 190°C., Gas Mark 5
Illustrated on page 19

Canadian tea loaf

Do not be put off by the carrot; it gives the loaf a lovely golden colour and nobody yet has guessed.

Imperial/Metric	American
7 oz./200 g. sugar	scant cup sugar
10 oz./275 g. plain flour	2½ cups all-purpose flour
pinch salt	pinch salt
¼ teaspoon bicarbonate of soda	¼ teaspoon baking soda
2 teaspoons baking powder	2 teaspoons baking powder
2 eggs	2 eggs
4 oz./100 g. carrots, finely grated	2 carrots, finely grated
½ teaspoon vanilla essence	½ teaspoon vanilla extract
scant ¼ pint/1½ dl. corn oil	½–⅔ cup corn oil
2 oz./50 g. walnuts, chopped	½ cup chopped walnuts
topping	topping
1 oz./25 g. butter	2 tablespoons butter
2 tablespoons soft brown sugar	3 tablespoons soft brown sugar
1 tablespoon milk	1 tablespoon milk
1 oz./25 g. walnuts, chopped	¼ cup chopped walnuts

Put all the dry ingredients in a large bowl and mix. Lightly beat the eggs and add to the bowl, stir well, add the carrot and vanilla, then slowly add the oil. Stir well, add the walnuts, stir, then put this rather sticky mixture in a well-greased 9- by 5-inch (23- by 13-cm.) loaf tin or make two small loaves, in which case reduce the cooking time. Bake in a moderate oven for about 50 minutes, or until the cake feels almost done. Ten minutes before it is done, put the topping ingredients in a small saucepan and heat gently until the sugar has melted. Remove the loaf from the oven and spoon on the topping, return to the oven for 10 minutes. Leave the loaf to cool in the tin. Cut in thick slices and serve buttered.

Cooking time about 1 hour
Oven temperature 350°F., 180°C., Gas Mark 4

Scones

Imperial/Metric	American
1 teaspoon salt	1 teaspoon salt
8 oz./225 g. self-raising flour	2 cups all-purpose flour sifted with 2 teaspoons baking powder
2 oz./50 g. margarine	¼ cup margarine
¼ pint/1½ dl. milk	⅔ cup milk

Add the salt to the flour and rub in the fat; add the liquid quickly, mixing with a knife. Gather the dough into a ball and put on to a floured board. Very lightly roll to about ½-inch (1-cm.) thickness and cut into rounds. If you are in a hurry, put the dough on to a greased baking tray and shape into a flattened round. Mark into triangles. Whatever you do, it is worth brushing the tops with a little beaten egg or milk. Cook in a hot to very hot oven for 10 minutes for the small scones, or in a hot oven for 30 minutes for the large one.

Cooking time small scones 10 minutes, large scone round 30 minutes
Oven temperature 450–475°F., 230–240°C., Gas Mark 8–9, or 425°F., 220°C., Gas Mark 7

Variations
Cheese scones Grate 2 oz. (50 g., ½ cup) cheese and add to the mixture with a pinch of dried mustard before adding the liquid. Put a little grated cheese on the top of each scone before cooking.
Fruit scones Add 1 oz. (25 g., 2 tablespoons) castor sugar to the flour before adding the margarine, and add 2 oz. (50 g., ⅓ cup) dried fruit before adding the liquid.

Biscuits and small cakes

Quick shortbread

Imperial/Metric	American
4 oz./100 g. margarine or butter	½ cup margarine or butter
2 oz./50 g. castor sugar	¼ cup granulated sugar
5 oz./150 g. plain flour	1¼ cups all-purpose flour
1 oz./25 g. ground rice	3 tablespoons ground rice
extra castor sugar	extra granulated sugar

Melt the margarine and sugar together in a saucepan. Remove from the heat and stir in the flour and ground rice. You can use 6 oz. (175 g., 1½ cups) flour instead if you haven't any ground rice. Mix well together and press into an 8-inch (20-cm.) flan tin. Prick with a fork all over and mark round the edge with the handle of a fork. Cook in a moderate oven for 40–50 minutes. Remove and allow to stand for 5 minutes before cutting into eight triangles. Dredge with extra castor sugar and leave to go cold before removing from the tin.

Cooking time 40–50 minutes
Oven temperature 325°F., 160°C., Gas Mark 3

Fudge biscuits

Imperial/Metric	American
4 oz./100 g. margarine	½ cup margarine
2 oz./50 g. icing sugar	½ cup sifted confectioners' sugar
4 oz./100 g. plain flour	1 cup all-purpose flour
2 tablespoons cocoa	3 tablespoons unsweetened cocoa powder

Cream the margarine and sugar together until soft and light. Add the flour and the cocoa and mix well together. Roll into 1-inch (2½-cm.) balls and place on a greased baking sheet. Press each ball flat with a fork which has been dipped in flour. Bake in a moderate oven for 10 minutes. Lift carefully on to a wire tray to cool.

Cooking time 10 minutes
Oven temperature 350°F., 180°C., Gas Mark 4

Almond macaroons

You can make these with an electric mixer, but somehow they seem much lighter if done by hand with a spoon.

Imperial/Metric	American
7 oz./200 g. castor sugar	1 cup granulated sugar
1 oz./25 g. granulated sugar	
4 oz./100 g. ground almonds	1 cup ground almonds
½ oz./15 g. ground rice	1½ tablespoons ground rice
2 egg whites	2 egg whites
½ teaspoon vanilla essence	½ teaspoon vanilla extract
rice paper	unglazed paper
split almonds	split almonds

Mix the sugars, ground almonds and rice together in a bowl. Add the egg whites and vanilla essence and beat together with a wooden spoon for about 5 minutes – very hard work but worth it! Leave to stand for 5 minutes and beat for a further 5 minutes, until thick and white. Lay the rice paper on to a baking tin and put teaspoonfuls of the mixture on to it, keeping them well apart. Put a split almond in the middle of each and cook in a moderate oven for 20–30 minutes.

Cooking time 20–30 minutes
Oven temperature 350°F., 180°C., Gas Mark 4

Chocolate biscuit cake

This is very fattening – but delicious! The children will love helping to crush the biscuits.

Imperial/Metric	American
8 oz./225 g. broken biscuits (include some ginger if possible)	2 cups cookie crumbs (include some ginger if possible)
4 oz./100 g. margarine	½ cup margarine
2 tablespoons golden syrup	3 tablespoons corn syrup
1 tablespoon cocoa	1 tablespoon unsweetened cocoa powder
4 oz./100 g. plain chocolate	⅔ cup semi-sweet chocolate pieces
few sultanas or raisins	few white or dark raisins

Crush the biscuits into crumbs with a rolling pin or milk bottle. Melt all the other ingredients together and add to the crushed biscuits. Stir well and pour into an 8-inch (20-cm.) flan tin. Smooth all over and put into the fridge for about 2 hours until hard.

Flapjacks

This recipe makes very light crunchy flapjacks and is easy to do, so that the children can help.

Imperial/Metric	American
4 oz./100 g. margarine	½ cup margarine
2 oz./50 g. granulated sugar	¼ cup granulated sugar
8 oz./225 g. rolled oats	2¼ cups rolled oats

Melt the margarine and the sugar together until really well mixed and bubbling. Add the oats and stir very well. Put into a greased Swiss roll tin and press down firmly. Mark into squares and press down again. Cook in a moderately hot oven for 10 minutes. Take out of the oven and mark into squares again. Leave to cool in the tin.

Cooking time 10 minutes
Oven temperature 375°F., 190°C., Gas Mark 5

Chocolate fudge date bars

Imperial/Metric	American
3 oz./75 g. self-raising flour	¾ cup all-purpose flour sifted with ¾ teaspoon baking powder
1 oz./25 g. cocoa	¼ cup unsweetened cocoa powder
3 oz./75 g. stoned dates	½ cup pitted dates
6 oz./175 g. soft light brown sugar	¾ cup soft light brown sugar
1 egg	1 egg
2 oz./50 g. margarine	¼ cup margarine
1 small can evaporated milk	1 small can evaporated milk
topping	topping
1 oz./25 g. margarine	2 tablespoons margarine
1 tablespoon cocoa	1 tablespoon unsweetened cocoa powder
7–8 oz./200–225 g. icing sugar	1½–1¾ cups sifted confectioners' sugar
few drops vanilla essence	few drops vanilla extract

Sieve the flour and cocoa together. Chop the dates and add to the flour with the sugar, lightly beaten egg and softened margarine. Mix well. Reserve 2 tablespoons evaporated milk from the tin and slowly add the rest to the mixture. Grease an 8- by 8- by 2-inch (20- by 20- by 5-cm.) square tin or 10- by 7-inch (25- by 18-cm.) oblong one. Pour the mixture into the tin and bake in a moderate oven for about 30 minutes. Leave the cake in the tin for 10 minutes after removing it from the oven, then turn out on to a wire rack. Leave to cool. To make the topping, put the margarine and cocoa in a saucepan, slowly add the remaining 2 tablespoons evaporated milk, then stir in the icing sugar and vanilla essence. Cook very gently for 4 minutes, then remove from the heat and beat very hard to thicken the mixture. Spread over the cake, and mark into pieces.

Cooking time about 35 minutes
Oven temperature 350°F., 180°C., Gas Mark 4

Matthew's ginger biscuits

Very good they are too!

Imperial/Metric	American
8 oz./225 g. soft dark brown sugar	**1 cup soft dark brown sugar**
$3\frac{1}{2}$ oz./100 g. rolled oats	**1 cup rolled oats**
4 oz./100 g. self-raising flour	**1 cup all-purpose flour sifted with 1 teaspoon baking powder**
1 teaspoon ground ginger	**1 teaspoon ground ginger**
1 teaspoon bicarbonate of soda	**1 teaspoon baking soda**
4 oz./100 g. margarine	**$\frac{1}{2}$ cup margarine**
2 tablespoons golden syrup	**3 tablespoons corn syrup**

Mix the dry ingredients together in a bowl. Melt the margarine and syrup together in a saucepan and add to the bowl. Stir well. Form into small balls with your hands (this bit the children will love!) and put on to a greased baking tin. Cook in a moderately hot oven for about 10 minutes. After 2 minutes cooking you may need to flatten them down a bit with your hand.
Cooking time about 10 minutes
Oven temperature 375–400°F., 190–200°C., Gas Mark 5–6

Brownies

This is a traditional American recipe.

Imperial/Metric	American
2 oz./50 g. unsweetened chocolate	**2 squares unsweetened chocolate**
4 oz./100 g. butter or margarine	**$\frac{1}{2}$ cup butter or margarine**
$3\frac{1}{2}$ oz./100 g. plain flour	**$\frac{3}{4}$ cup plus 2 tablespoons all-purpose flour**
$\frac{1}{2}$ teaspoon baking powder	**$\frac{1}{2}$ teaspoon baking powder**
$\frac{1}{4}$ teaspoon salt	**$\frac{1}{4}$ teaspoon salt**
2 eggs	**2 eggs**
$6\frac{1}{2}$ oz./185 g. sugar	**$\frac{3}{4}$ cup plus 1 tablespoon sugar**
1 teaspoon vanilla essence	**1 teaspoon vanilla extract**
2–3 oz./50–75 g. walnuts, coarsely chopped	**$\frac{1}{2}$–$\frac{3}{4}$ cup coarsely chopped walnuts**

Preheat the oven to moderate. Lightly grease an 8- by 8- by 2-inch (20- by 20- by 5-cm.) baking tin. Put the chocolate with the butter into a small basin and melt them over hot water. You can do this in a saucepan, but watch it very carefully to see it doesn't stick. Cool. Sift the flour, baking powder and salt together and set aside. In a large bowl, using either a wooden spoon or a mixer at medium speed, beat the eggs and sugar together until light. Beat in the chocolate mixture and vanilla essence. Stir in the flour and the nuts. Pour into the prepared tin and spread out evenly. Bake for 25–30 minutes. Let cool for 10 minutes and cut into squares with a sharp knife. Leave to go cold in the tin. These taste marvellous with ice cream.
Cooking time 25–30 minutes
Oven temperature 350°F., 180°C., Gas Mark 4

Jam or lemon curd tarts

Making these will keep most small children happy for hours. Make up a small quantity of shortcrust pastry, grease some tart tins, roll out the pastry $\frac{1}{8}$–$\frac{1}{4}$ inch ($\frac{1}{4}$–$\frac{1}{2}$ cm.) thick and cut into rounds a little larger than the tins. Put the pastry rounds in the tins. Put a good teaspoonful of jam or lemon curd in each, cover with half a teaspoon of water and bake in a hot oven (425°F., 220°C., Gas Mark 7) for 10–15 minutes.

Florentine fingers

These are far less trouble to make than the real thing.

Imperial/Metric	American
4 oz./100 g. plain chocolate	**$\frac{2}{3}$ cup semi-sweet chocolate pieces**
2 oz./50 g. glacé cherries	**$\frac{1}{4}$ cup candied cherries**
2 oz./50 g. margarine	**$\frac{1}{4}$ cup margarine**
4 oz./100 g. castor sugar	**$\frac{1}{2}$ cup granulated sugar**
1 egg	**1 egg**
2 oz./50 g. raisins	**$\frac{1}{3}$ cup raisins**
1 oz./25 g. flaked almonds or chopped walnuts	**3 tablespoons flaked almonds or chopped walnuts**
4 oz./100 g. desiccated coconut	**$1\frac{1}{3}$ cups shredded coconut**

Melt the chocolate over hot water and spread over the base of an approximately 8-inch (20-cm.) square tin. Roughly chop the cherries. Cream the margarine and sugar, add the beaten egg and stir in the cherries, raisins, nuts and coconut. Spread over the chocolate and bake in a moderate oven for 30

minutes. Cool, then cut into fingers.
Cooking time 30 minutes
Oven temperature 350°F., 180°C., Gas Mark 4

Chocolate date krisps

Imperial/Metric	American
1 8-oz./227-g. packet dates	1⅓ cups dates
2 oz./50 g. margarine	¼ cup margarine
2 oz./50 g. castor sugar	¼ cup granulated sugar
3 oz./75 g. rice krispies	3 cups rice krispies
4–6 oz./100–175 g. cooking chocolate	⅔–1 cup semi-sweet chocolate pieces

Chop the dates. Melt the margarine, then remove from the heat and add the sugar, then the dates and rice krispies. Put into a greased 8-inch (20-cm.) square tin and when cold pour melted chocolate over the mixture. When the chocolate is getting firm mark into squares.
Illustrated on page 51

Almond slices

Imperial/Metric	American
6 oz./175 g. shortcrust pastry	basic pie dough made with 1½ cups flour
filling	filling
4 oz./100 g. castor sugar	1 cup sifted confectioners' sugar
1½–2 oz./40–50 g. margarine	3–4 tablespoons margarine
4 oz./100 g. ground rice	⅔ cup ground rice
1 egg	1 egg
almond essence	almond extract
raspberry jam	raspberry jam
flaked almonds	flaked almonds

First bake a pastry case in a long narrow tin, a Swiss roll tin will do.
   Cream the sugar, margarine and ground rice together in a bowl. Add the beaten egg, and then the almond essence to taste; you will find you need quite a lot of this. Spread the base of the pastry case with raspberry jam and cover with the almond filling. Sprinkle some flaked almonds on the top and bake in a moderate oven for 25 minutes. Allow to cool, and cut into slices.
Cooking time 25 minutes
Oven temperature 350°F., 180°C., Gas Mark 4

Butterscotch brownies

Imperial/Metric	American
4 oz./100 g. margarine	½ cup margarine
6 oz./175 g. soft brown	¾ cup soft brown sugar
1 egg	1 egg
½ teaspoon vanilla essence	½ teaspoon vanilla extract
5 oz./150 g. plain flour	1¼ cups all-purpose flour
1 teaspoon baking powder	1 teaspoon baking powder
pinch salt	pinch salt
2 oz./50 g. walnuts, chopped	½ cup chopped walnuts

Melt the margarine, remove from the heat, stir in the brown sugar, cool, then beat in the egg and vanilla. Sift together the flour, baking powder and salt, stir into the sugar mixture, then add the nuts and stir well. Spread into an 8- by 8- by 2-inch (20- by 20- by 5-cm.) square tin and bake in a moderate oven for 20–25 minutes. Leave to cool in the tin and when cool cut into squares. Good with vanilla ice cream and butterscotch sauce (see page 30).
Cooking time 20–25 minutes
Oven temperature 350°F., 180°C., Gas Mark 4

Quick cookie bars

These really take only a few minutes to make and there is no mixing. Children enjoy helping with these.

Imperial/Metric	American
2 oz./50 g. glacé cherries	¼ cup candied cherries
4 oz./100 g. margarine	½ cup margarine
4 oz./100 g. porridge oats	generous cup rolled oats
6 oz./175 g. sultanas	1 cup white raisins
3 oz./75 g. desiccated coconut	1 cup shredded coconut
1 large can condensed milk	1 large can condensed milk

Roughly chop the cherries. Put the chopped margarine in a shallow oblong tin, a Swiss roll tin is perfect. Put the tin in the oven until the margarine has melted, then sprinkle the oats evenly into the tin, sprinkle the sultanas over the oats, then the cherries and coconut. Pour the condensed milk over the whole lot and bake in a moderate oven for 25–30 minutes until golden brown. Leave to cool in the tin then cut into bars.
Cooking time 25–30 minutes
Oven temperature 350°F., 180°C., Gas Mark 4

Cakes

Basic sandwich cake

Do try to use one of the soft margarines for these cakes, and bake as soon as the mixture is ready. You can alter the quantities to 4 oz. flour, margarine and sugar and 2 eggs, if you want a smaller cake.

Imperial/Metric	American
6 oz./175 g. margarine	¾ cup margarine
3 eggs	3 eggs
6 oz./175 g. self-raising flour	1½ cups all-purpose flour sifted with 1½ teaspoons baking powder
pinch salt	pinch salt
6 oz./175 g. castor sugar	¾ cup granulated sugar
3 tablespoons milk	4 tablespoons milk

Grease two 7-inch (18-cm.) tins. Roughly chop the margarine and put all the ingredients in a large mixing bowl. Beat for 2 minutes with an electric mixer, scrape the bowl, then beat again for 1 minute. Spread the mixture into the tins and bake in a moderately hot oven for 20–25 minutes. Turn out to cool on a wire rack. Try it in an 8-inch (20-cm.) square tin for a change.

Cooking time 20–25 minutes
Oven temperature 375°F., 190°C., Gas Mark 5

Variations

This very basic cake mixture can very easily be transformed into one of the following:

Orange layer cake Add the finely grated rind and the juice of 1 orange instead of the milk. Put orange butter icing (see page 50) in the centre and orange glacé icing (see page 50) on the top.

Chocolate cake Add 4 tablespoons (⅓ cup) cocoa and a small pinch of bicarbonate of soda with the flour, plus ¼ teaspoon vanilla essence or 1 teaspoon instant coffee. Ice with chocolate or coffee icing (see page 50) or try apricot jam in the centre and chocolate glacé icing (see page 50) on the top. Try topping the all-chocolate cake with sliced Mars bars and a crumbled flaky bar.

Coffee cake Mix 1 tablespoon instant coffee with 1 tablespoon hot water and add to the mixture, using 1 tablespoon less milk. Ice with coffee butter icing (see page 50) to which you have added a few chopped walnuts; top with coffee glacé icing (see page 50) and walnut halves.

Whelan's whacky cake

Once you have this recipe, all those excuses like 'I'm no good at making cakes', and, 'I just didn't have time', can no longer be used with complete honesty. It works! This is also rather good eaten as a pudding, warm, with vanilla or chocolate sauce. If you have a loose-bottomed tin it makes it easier to turn out.

Imperial/Metric	American
8 oz./225 g. plain flour	2 cups all-purpose flour
7 oz./200 g. castor sugar	scant cup granulated sugar
2 oz./50 g. cocoa	½ cup unsweetened cocoa powder
1 teaspoon bicarbonate of soda	1 teaspoon baking soda
1 teaspoon salt	1 teaspoon salt
1 teaspoon vanilla essence	1 teaspoon vanilla extract
1 teaspoon vinegar	1 teaspoon vinegar
5 tablespoons corn oil	6 tablespoons corn oil
7½ fl. oz./2 dl. water	scant cup water

Mix together the flour, sugar and cocoa and sift into an ungreased 8-inch (20-cm.) square baking tin. Make three holes in the top of the dry ingredients. Into the first put the bicarbonate of soda and salt, into the second the vanilla and vinegar, into the third put the corn oil. Over the whole thing pour the cold water. Stir gently until smooth and bake in a moderate oven for 35 minutes.

Cooking time 35 minutes
Oven temperature 350°F., 180°C., Gas Mark 4

Boiled fruit cake

This is the best and easiest method I know of making a really good fruit cake.

Imperial/Metric	American
1 breakfast cup each sugar, sultanas, raisins, currants and water	1 cup each sugar, white raisins, dark raisins, currants and water
2 teaspoons mixed peel	2 teaspoons mixed candied peel
8 oz./225 g. margarine	1 cup margarine
1 teaspoon mixed spice	1 teaspoon mixed spice
pinch salt	pinch salt
2 eggs, beaten	2 eggs, beaten
8 oz./225 g. self-raising flour	2 cups all-purpose flour sifted with 2 teaspoons baking powder

Place everything except the eggs and flour in a large saucepan, bring to the boil and cook gently for 15–20 minutes. Leave to cool *really* thoroughly, preferably overnight. Stir in the eggs and flour and put into a 7-inch (18-cm.) round, loose-bottomed tin. Bake in a moderate oven for about 2 hours. It is a good idea to cover the top of the cake with foil or greaseproof paper after 1 hour to prevent burning.

Cooking time about 2 hours

Oven temperature 325°F., 160°C., Gas Mark 3

Coffee cream puffs

These are a bit of a fiddle to make, but one mouthful is enough to convince us they are worth it!

Imperial/Metric	American
choux pastry	choux paste
2½ oz./65 g. plain flour	⅔ cup all-purpose flour
pinch salt	pinch salt
¼ pint/1½ dl. water	⅔ cup water
2 oz./50 g. margarine or butter	¼ cup margarine or butter
2 eggs, beaten	2 eggs, beaten
filling	filling
½ pint/3 dl. cream, whipped	1¼ cups cream, whipped
little icing sugar	little confectioners' sugar
topping	topping
coffee glacé icing (see page 50)	coffee glacé icing (see page 50)

Sift the flour and salt twice. Put the water and margarine in a saucepan and heat gently until the margarine melts, then boil briskly. As soon as it is boiling take it off the heat and add the flour all at once. Beat hard until the mixture forms a soft ball and leaves the sides of the pan. Cool until you can stand the saucepan on the back of your hand comfortably. Add the eggs gradually and beat hard until the mixture is smooth and glossy and stands in soft peaks. Spoon or pipe 16 equal amounts of the pastry on to a well-buttered tray and bake in a moderately hot oven for 10 minutes. Lower the heat to moderate and bake for a further 20 minutes until well puffed and golden. Remove from the oven, make a small slit in each and put back to dry out for 5 minutes. Cool on a wire rack. When really cold split in half and fill with the cream, sweetened with a little icing sugar. Ice with glacé icing, fall into a chair and eat one!

Cooking time 35 minutes

Oven temperature 400°F., 200°C., Gas Mark 6, then 350°F., 180°C., Gas Mark 4

Pineapple and coconut sponge

Imperial/Metric	American
cake	cake
6 oz./175 g. self-raising flour	1½ cups all-purpose flour sifted with 1½ teaspoons baking powder
6 oz./175 g. soft margarine	¾ cup soft margarine
6 oz./175 g. castor sugar	¾ cup granulated sugar
3 eggs	3 eggs
2–3 tablespoons pineapple juice	3–4 tablespoons pineapple juice
topping	topping
1 13¼-oz./376-g. can crushed pineapple or 1 12-oz./240-g. can kiddy cubes	1 13¼-oz. can crushed pineapple or tiny cubes
1 oz./25 g. margarine	2 tablespoons margarine
2 oz./50 g. soft brown sugar	¼ cup soft brown sugar
2 oz./50 g. desiccated coconut	⅔ cup shredded coconut
glacé cherries	candied cherries

Strain the pineapple for the topping, reserving the juice for the cake. Preheat the oven to moderate. Put all the ingredients for the cake in a bowl and beat, preferably with an electric mixer, until the mixture is thick, pale and creamy. Grease an 8-inch (20-cm.) square tin and carefully spoon in the mixture. Cook for 25–30 minutes. Remove the cake from the tin and leave on a rack to cool. Put the cake upside down on to a heatproof plate or baking tray. To make the topping, melt the margarine, add the sugar and when this has dissolved add the strained pineapple and the coconut. Remove from the heat and mix well. Heat the grill. Spoon the mixture over the cake, decorate with a few cherries and put under the grill for a few minutes to toast the coconut and slightly colour the pineapple.

Cooking time 25–30 minutes

Oven temperature 375°F., 190°C., Gas Mark 5

Illustrated on page 23

Pam's apple shortcake

The one essential for this cake is an 8-inch (20-cm.) tin with removable sides or base.

Imperial/Metric shortcake	American shortcake
6 oz./175 g. margarine	¾ cup margarine
4 oz./100 g. castor sugar	½ cup granulated sugar
1 egg	1 egg
8 oz./225 g. flour	2 cups flour
2 teaspoons baking powder	2 teaspoons baking powder
filling	filling
2–3 lb./1–1¼ kg. apples	2–3 lb. apples
2 oz./50 g. castor sugar, or to taste	¼ cup granulated sugar, or to taste
1 teaspoon cinnamon or few cloves	1 teaspoon cinnamon or few cloves
icing sugar	confectioners' sugar

To make the shortcake, cream the margarine and sugar, add the lightly beaten egg and stir in the flour and baking powder. Line the cake tin with this mixture, pressing it into place with a spatula or your hands and reserving a third of the mixture for the lid. For the filling, peel, core and coarsely grate or very thinly slice the apples; mix with the sugar and the cinnamon (much nicer than cloves for this). Pack the apples into the tin. Flatten the remaining mixture with floured hands into a circle, cut into four and place on top of the apples to form a lid, leaving a large hole in the centre. Seal the edges together well. Bake in a moderate oven for about 1 hour; the exact time depends on the quantity of apples used. Allow to cool for 15 minutes before removing from the tin; sprinkle with sieved icing sugar and serve with lightly whipped cream.

Cooking time about 1 hour
Oven temperature 350°F., 180°C., Gas Mark 4

Fruit gâteau

Imperial/Metric	American
3 eggs	3 eggs
4 oz./100 g. castor sugar	½ cup granulated sugar
3 oz./75 g. self-raising flour	¾ cup all-purpose flour
1 teaspoon baking powder	1¾ teaspoons baking powder
½ pint/3 dl. double cream	1¼ cups whipping cream
fresh, frozen or canned fruit	fresh, frozen or canned fruit

Beat the eggs with the sugar until really thick and creamy. Sift the flour with the baking powder and carefully fold into the mixture using a metal spoon. Grease and flour two 7-inch sandwich tins and spoon in the mixture. Smooth over the top leaving a slight hollow in the centre. Bake in a moderately hot oven for 15–20 minutes. Remove from the tins and leave on a rack to cool.

Beat the cream until stiff. Roughly chop some of the fruit. Remove a little cream from the bowl then fold in the fruit. Use the fruit cream mixture for the centre of the cake. Taste it first to see if it needs a little castor sugar. Decorate the top of the cake with the remaining cream and some whole strawberries or raspberries or sliced peaches.

Cooking time 15–20 minutes
Oven temperature 375°F., 190°C., Gas Mark 5

Apple cake

Imperial/Metric	American
1 3-egg basic sandwich cake mixture (see page 46)	1 3-egg basic sandwich cake batter (see page 46)
filling	filling
1 lb./450 g. cooking apples, sliced thinly	1 lb. cooking apples, sliced thinly
4 oz./100 g. soft brown sugar	½ cup soft brown sugar
few raisins or sultanas	few dark or white raisins
½ teaspoon cinnamon	½ teaspoon cinnamon
streusel topping	streusel topping
1½ oz./40 g. butter	3 tablespoons butter
2 oz./50 g. flour	½ cup flour
2 oz./50 g. soft brown sugar	¼ cup soft brown sugar

Make up the basic sandwich cake mixture. To make the filling, mix together the sliced apples, sugar, raisins and cinnamon. Grease an 8-inch (20-cm.) square tin, put half the mixture in the tin, cover with the apples, and cover this with the remaining cake mixture. To make the topping, rub the butter into the flour, add the sugar and sprinkle over the cake before baking. Bake in a moderately hot oven for 45–55 minutes. Leave the cake to cool for a few minutes before turning out. For a simpler cake, omit the topping and sprinkle the cooked cake with sugar before serving.

Cooking time 45–55 minutes
Oven temperature 375°F., 190°C., Gas Mark 5

Children's parties

Children's parties have changed considerably over the years as children's tastes have become more sophisticated. Nowadays children will almost always choose a sausage on a stick rather than a jam sandwich. At parties, children would much rather stuff themselves with crisps, twiglets and the like, all of which are much easier to buy than to make at home! In some funny way, savouries seem to have more prestige attached to them in the children's eyes if they come out of a packet. This also applies to any form of chocolate biscuit that comes individually wrapped in silver paper – the paper being more important to them than the biscuit! So don't waste your energy trying to make these. However, barring the unpredictable, the highlight of the party should be the cake. All but one of our recipes start with the basic sandwich cake given on page 46, preferably flavoured with chocolate or coffee. Decoration is all important, and we have given seven easy-to-follow ideas with diagrams. Whichever you do, use every opportunity to add as many sweets as possible. This is the secret of success! We have included a few other ideas, such as Smartie cakes. Sandwiches we leave up to you, but do cut them very small, remove the crusts, and make the fillings simple, and easy to recognise. Jelly and ice cream, the more brightly coloured the better, are still favourites. However, knowing that sheer high spirits can chip cups and smash plates, we always use colourful plastic or paper ones which have the additional advantage of eliminating washing up. With the exception of the ice cream, all our suggestions for parties can be eaten in the fingers, young children being both clumsy and dangerous with knives and forks.

Birthday cakes

Very small children are usually happy with a simple cake and candles to blow out. It is very easy to make a plain round cake into a clock face, using icing or sweets to write the numbers, and pointing the hands to the child's age. A duck pond, using plastic ducks and a piece of foil, is simple too; or stand chocolate bears round the outside of the cake with one on top holding Smartie 'balloons' by icing 'strings'. Sugar mice on the top is another favourite, and the following are some ideas which are very easy to copy.

Vanilla glacé icing

Imperial/Metric	American
8 oz./225 g. sifted icing sugar	2 cups sifted confectioners' sugar
1½ tablespoons hot water	2 tablespoons hot water
½ teaspoon vanilla essence	½ teaspoon vanilla extract

Put the sugar into a bowl and gradually add the water and vanilla. Stir hard until smooth and thick enough to coat the back of a spoon. Add more water or icing sugar if necessary.

Variations

Coffee glacé icing Dissolve 2 teaspoons coffee powder in the hot water or add 2 teaspoons coffee essence and 1 tablespoon hot water.

Chocolate glacé icing Dissolve 2 tablespoons cocoa in the hot water and add ½ oz. (15 g., 1 tablespoon) butter before adding the sugar.

Orange or lemon glacé icing Add 1 teaspoon finely grated orange or lemon rind to the sugar. Mix with strained and warmed juice instead of water.

Butter icings Use exactly the same method but add 2 oz. (50 g., ¼ cup) butter or margarine and substitute milk (or orange juice, coffee, etc.) for the water.

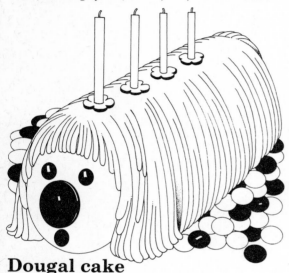

Dougal cake

Imperial/Metric	American
1 3-egg chocolate basic sandwich cake mixture (see page 46)	**1 3-egg chocolate basic sandwich cake batter (see page 46)**
icing	frosting
3 oz./75 g. soft margarine	**6 tablespoons soft margarine**
2 tablespoons coffee essence	**3 tablespoons coffee flavoring**
1 teaspoon boiling water	**1 teaspoon boiling water**
8–12 oz./225–350 g. icing sugar	**2–3 cups sifted confectioners' sugar**
decoration	decoration
1 large oval meringue	**1 large oval meringue**
1 packet Smarties	**1 package m & m's**
1 oval chocolate	**1 oval chocolate candy**

First make the cake, by putting all the ingredients together in a bowl and beating well for 2–3 minutes. Put into a greased and floured 2-lb. (1-kg.) loaf tin

and bake in a moderately hot oven for 30–40 minutes, until the top is firm to the touch. Allow to cool for a minute or two, and turn out on to a wire tray to cool. Meanwhile make the icing by beating the margarine, coffee essence and boiling water together in a bowl. Gradually add the icing sugar until the icing is of a soft consistency, but not too runny.

Place the cake on a plate and level the top off, sloping the sides slightly. Completely cover with the icing. Stick the meringue on the front for a face. With a fork, make a parting down the middle of the back and fork lines down the sides, as if it were hair. Put a blob on the end for a tail and 'comb' a little icing round the sides of the meringue and on the top to look like a fringe. Using a tiny bit of icing, stick two brown Smarties on to the meringue for eyes, the oval chocolate for a nose, and a red Smartie for the tongue.

Put the remainder of the packet of Smarties round the edge of the plate to look like flowers.

Cooking time 30–40 minutes

Oven temperature 375°F., 190°C., Gas Mark 5

Treasure chest

Imperial/Metric	American
1 3-egg chocolate basic sandwich cake mixture (see page 46)	**1 3-egg chocolate basic sandwich cake batter (see page 46)**
icing	frosting
2 recipes chocolate butter icing (see page 50)	**2 recipes chocolate butter icing (see page 50)**
little vanilla glacé icing (see page 49)	**little vanilla glacé icing (see page 49)**
decoration	decoration
2 small biscuits	**2 small cookies**
sweets	**candies**
gold-covered chocolate money	**gold-covered chocolate money**

Bake the cake in a 2-lb. (1-kg.) loaf tin. When cold cut a slice off the top to form a lid about ½ inch (1 cm.) deep. Ice the base and the top and sides of the lid with the chocolate icing and put the base on a cake board. Replace the lid, propping it open with two small biscuits at the back. Fill the gap with chocolate money. Using a plain nozzle and an icing bag, ice bands on to the chest with vanilla glacé icing. When almost dry, stick jelly sweets on the bands as 'jewels' and put more money in front of the cake as though it is tumbling out of the chest.

Cooking time 30–40 minutes

Oven temperature 375°F., 190°C., Gas Mark 5

Illustrated opposite

Chocolate crisp ice cream (page 57), chocolate date krisps (page 45), frozen lemon crunch (page 29), corn crisps (page 57) and treasure chest cake

House

Imperial/Metric
**1 6-egg coffee basic
    sandwich cake
    mixture (see
    page 46)**
icing
**2 recipes chocolate
    butter icing
    (see page 50)**
**1 recipe vanilla glacé
    icing (see page 50)**
decoration
**3 packets chocolate
    buttons**
**1 chocolate wafer
    biscuit**
angelica
jelly tots or Smarties

American
**1 6-egg coffee basic
    sandwich cake
    batter (see
    page 46)**
frosting
**2 recipes chocolate
    butter icing
    (see page 50)**
**1 recipe vanilla glacé
    icing (see page 50)**
decoration
**3 packages chocolate
    mint wafers**
**1 chocolate wafer
    cookie**
candied angelica
jelly beans or m & m's

Make two 8-inch (20-cm.) square coffee cakes, with
two-thirds of the mixture in one and one-third in the
other. When cold, cut the large cake in half and sandwich one half on top of the other with some of the
chocolate icing.

To make the roof, cut a triangular section from
the middle of the second cake and lay it along the
centre of the house. Make a tent over the top with the
remaining two pieces, see diagram.

To decorate, cover the roof with chocolate icing
and put chocolate buttons all over like tiles. Cut a
triangle shape out of one end of the chocolate biscuit
and fit the biscuit over the roof for a chimney. Allow
the roof to dry a little. Cover the rest of the house
with white icing and, using a small plain nozzle and
an icing bag, draw on windows and a front door with
remaining chocolate icing. Decorate as you like
with angelica and sweets for climbing roses, etc.
Cooking time large cake 40–50 minutes, smaller
cake 25–30 minutes
Oven temperature 375°F., 190°C., Gas Mark 5

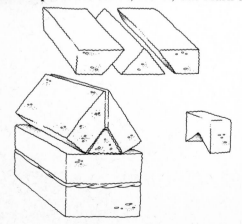

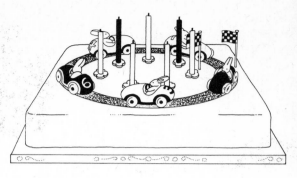

Race track

Imperial/Metric
**1 3-egg orange or
    lemon basic
    sandwich cake
    mixture (see page 46)**
**1 large oblong board
    or foil-covered
    baking tray**
icing
**1 recipe orange or
    lemon butter
    icing (see page 50)**
decoration
**3 oz./75 g. desiccated
    coconut**
little green colouring

small racing cars
candles and holders
**cocktail sticks and
    paper to make flags**
**plastic or wooden
    people**

American
**1 3-egg orange or
    lemon basic
    sandwich cake
    batter (see page 46)**
**1 large oblong board
    or foil-covered
    baking tray**
frosting
**1 recipe orange or
    lemon butter
    icing (see page 50)**
decoration
**1 cup shredded
    coconut**
**little green food
    coloring**

small racing cars
candles and holders
**toothpicks and paper
    to make flags**
**plastic or wooden
    people**

Bake the cake in a Swiss roll tin. Put the cake on a
board or baking tray and cover with the icing. Mix
2 oz. (50 g., ⅔ cup) of the coconut with green colouring
for grass. Lightly toast the remaining coconut for
the track. Spoon the toasted coconut on to the cake
in a large oval to make the track, then put the green
coconut on the top and sides of the cake. Put cars
on the track, candles in the centre and make two
chequered flags for the finish. Place a few people
around the track. You can elaborate on this with
railings made of chocolate matchsticks, a grand-
stand made from chocolate biscuits, etc. If it is a
small party each of the children can be given one of
the racing cars.
Cooking time 20–25 minutes
Oven temperature 375°F., 190°C., Gas Mark 5

Rocket

Imperial/Metric	American
1 2-egg chocolate or vanilla basic sandwich cake mixture (see page 46)	**1 2-egg chocolate or vanilla basic sandwich cake batter (see page 46)**
1 chocolate Swiss roll	**1 chocolate cream roll**
1 7-inch (18-cm.) cake board, or bread board covered with foil	**1 7-inch cake board, or bread board covered with foil**
icing	frosting
2 recipes chocolate butter icing (see page 50)	**2 recipes chocolate butter icing (see page 50)**
decoration	decoration
small packet sugar stars cereal	**small package sugar stars cereal**
miniature chocolate Swiss rolls, 1 for each year of child's age	**chocolate Ho-Ho's, 1 for each year of child's age**
candles and holders	**candles and holders**
5-inch (13-cm.) circle of cardboard (cut from cereal packet) covered with foil	**5-inch circle of cardboard (cut from cereal package) covered with foil**

Bake the cake in a 6-inch (15-cm.) tin. When cold, put the sponge cake on the board and hollow the centre enough to make the Swiss roll stand up. Spread the chocolate icing over both cakes, saving a little to stick a few sugar stars on to the Swiss roll. Stand the miniature Swiss rolls around the cake and put a candle in the top of each. Make the cardboard into a cone by cutting into the centre then folding one side over and sticking it down. Put it on top of the Swiss roll (see diagram).
Cooking time 35–40 minutes
Oven temperature 375°F., 190°C., Gas Mark 5

Train

There is no cooking with this cake. It is a very good idea for small children.

Imperial/Metric	American
8 miniature chocolate Swiss rolls, or 1 per child and 2 extra	**8 chocolate Ho-Ho's, or 1 per child and 2 extra**
1 recipe chocolate butter icing (see page 50)	**1 recipe chocolate butter icing (see page 50)**
1 jelly sweet for funnel	**1 jelly candy for funnel**
2 packets Refreshers or Polos	**2 packages Life-savers**
1 12-inch (30-cm.) silver cake board	**1 12-inch silver cake board**
uncooked long spaghetti or plastic straws	**uncooked long spaghetti or plastic straws**
small wooden toys	**small wooden toys**
Smarties and other sweets	**m & m's and other candies**

First make the engine by cutting one miniature chocolate Swiss roll in half and sticking one of the cut halves on end on top of a second whole mini-roll, using the icing. Add the jelly sweet for a funnel at the front. To make the carriages, stick on four 'wheels' of Refreshers or Polos on each of the mini-rolls left, using icing. Assemble round the edge of the board, using spaghetti or cut plastic straws as couplings. Using small wooden toys, make a village or station in the centre of the board, sprinkling extra sweets in amongst the houses. Give one carriage to each child.

Maypole

Imperial/Metric	American
1 3-egg orange basic sandwich cake mixture (see page 46)	1 3-egg orange basic sandwich cake batter (see page 46)
icing	frosting
1 recipe orange butter icing (see page 50)	1 recipe orange butter icing (see page 50)
1–2 recipes orange glacé icing (see page 50)	1–2 recipes orange glacé icing (see page 50)
decoration	decoration
piece of beading or bamboo for the pole	**piece of bamboo or a candy cane for the pole**
few pieces of pink and blue ribbon	**few pieces of pink and blue ribbon**
different coloured ribbon to make streamers	**different colored ribbon to make streamers**
few pieces of stiff paper and some pins	**few pieces of stiff paper and some pins**

Bake the cake in an 8-inch (20-cm.) round tin. When cold, split and fill with the orange butter icing and ice the sides and top with orange glacé icing. Wind the pink and blue ribbon around the pole and stand in the centre of the cake. Take one coloured ribbon for each child, wind round the top, fix with a piece of sellotape if necessary, then bring out to the edge of the cake. Fold small pieces of paper over to stand up, write each child's name on a piece of paper and pin one to the end of each piece of ribbon so that they stand up around the cake. To make even prettier, pin a few artificial forget-me-nots or other small flowers to the maypole.

Cooking time 25–30 minutes
Oven temperature 375°F., 190°C., Gas Mark 5

Party food
Cheese and chive dip

Imperial/Metric	American
6 oz./175 g. Philadelphia or other cream cheese	**¾ cup Philadelphia or other cream cheese**
3 tablespoons cream	**¼ cup cream**
2 tablespoons chopped chives	**3 tablespoons chopped chives**
salt and pepper	**salt and pepper**

Beat all the ingredients together until smooth, adding more cream if necessary. Serve in a bowl surrounded with small cracker biscuits and twiglets for the children to dip in.

Marmite and cheese wheels

Imperial/Metric	American
1 packet frozen puff pastry	**1 package frozen puff paste or puff paste mix**
Marmite	**Marmite (optional)**
2 oz./50 g. Cheddar cheese, grated	**½ cup grated Cheddar cheese**

Roll the pastry to an oblong about 12 by 8 inches (30 by 20 cm.). Dab quite generously with Marmite and sprinkle with the grated cheese. Carefully roll up tightly, starting with one of the long sides. Dampen the edge with a little cold water to make it stick. Cut into thin slices. Place the slices on a greased baking sheet and cook in a hot oven for 10 minutes or until golden brown. Try to warm these before eating as they taste much better. This is another recipe the children will enjoy helping with.

Cooking time 10 minutes
Oven temperature 425°F., 220°C., Gas Mark 7

Cheese straws

Imperial/Metric	American
6 oz./175 g. plain flour	**1½ cups all-purpose flour**
4 oz./100 g. margarine	**½ cup margarine**
4 oz./100 g. Cheddar cheese, grated	**1 cup grated Cheddar cheese**
salt and pepper	**salt and pepper**
1 egg	**1 egg**

Put the flour in a large bowl, chop the margarine, rub in with the fingers until the mixture is crumbly, then add the cheese and salt and pepper. Lightly beat the egg and add to the flour mixture with a knife,

Two-way stretch: fish pie (page 33) and scalloped fish (page 34)

mixing together until it binds. Shape into a ball and wrap in polythene; chill for 30 minutes. Turn on to a floured board, roll out until the mixture is ¼ inch (½ cm.) thick, cut into straws and place on a greased baking tray. Bake in a moderately hot oven for 8 minutes or until golden. Cool on a wire rack.

Cooking time 8 minutes
Oven temperature 400°F., 200°C., Gas Mark 6

Special sausage rolls

Imperial/Metric	American
4 oz./100 g. margarine	½ cup margarine
4 oz./100 g. cream cheese	½ cup cream cheese
6 oz./175 g. plain flour	1½ cups all-purpose flour
pinch salt	pinch salt
8 oz./225 g. pork sausage meat	1 cup pork sausage meat
little milk	little milk

Chop the margarine into small pieces in a large bowl, add the cream cheese, flour and salt and chop all together with a knife until well blended. Gather into a ball by hand and put in a polythene bag in the fridge for 1 hour. Roll out on a floured board into one or two long narrow strips, ¼ inch (½ cm.) thick. Grease a large baking tray. Roll the sausage meat by hand into one or two long sausage shapes, the same length as the pastry. Put the sausage meat on the pastry and fold the pastry over to make one long sausage roll. Trim edges of the pastry, knock edges together with the back of a knife, brush with a little milk, cut into the required size and place the rolls on the baking tray. Bake in a hot oven for 20–25 minutes or until golden brown. Cool on a wire tray.

Cooking time 20–25 minutes
Oven temperature 425°F., 220°C., Gas Mark 7

Min's lemonade

Imperial/Metric	American
2 lemons	2 lemons
1 lb./450 g. granulated sugar	2 cups granulated sugar
½ oz./15 g. tartaric acid	5 teaspoons tartaric acid
2 pints/generous litre boiling water	5 cups boiling water

Grate the rinds of the lemons and squeeze the lemon halves. Put the rind and juice with the sugar and tartaric acid in a large jug or basin. Pour over the boiling water, stir well and leave for 12 hours. Strain and dilute to taste. This can very easily be doubled.

Nut crescents

Imperial/Metric	American
3 oz./75 g. almonds, chopped and roasted	¾ cup chopped and roasted almonds
7 oz./200 g. margarine	1 cup less 2 tablespoons margarine
8 oz./225 g. plain flour	2 cups all-purpose flour
2 oz./50 g. castor sugar	¼ cup granulated sugar
icing sugar	confectioners' sugar

To roast the almonds, put them into a tin in a low oven for a few minutes until they are golden brown. Put all the ingredients except the icing sugar into the mixer and mix into a paste. Roll the paste into little balls then into sausage shapes and finally into crescent shapes. Bake on greaseproof paper which has been oiled in a moderately hot oven for about 20 minutes until pale gold. Cool and roll them in icing sugar.

Cooking time 20 minutes
Oven temperature 350°F., 180°C., Gas Mark 4

Domino biscuits

Imperial/Metric	American
4 oz./100 g. semi-sweet biscuits	1 cup graham cracker crumbs
3 tablespoons chocolate spread	¼ cup chocolate spread or melted chocolate
1 tablespoon clear honey	1 tablespoon clear honey
4 oz./100 g. soft margarine	½ cup soft margarine
2 oz./50 g. icing sugar	½ cup sifted confectioners' sugar

Crush the biscuits finely. Put the chocolate spread, honey, and 3 oz. (75 g., 6 tablespoons) of the margarine into a saucepan. Melt, stirring frequently. Stir the chocolate mixture into the biscuits and mix well. Pour into a greased 7-inch (18-cm.) square tin and leave to set in the fridge. Cut into 24 oblong pieces. Put the icing sugar into a bowl and add the remaining 1 oz. (25 g., 2 tablespoons) margarine. Beat together until fluffy. Add a few drops of warm water and beat until smooth. Put the icing into a forcing bag with a plain small nozzle fitted. Pipe a line across each biscuit and dots to represent dominoes. If the child is five, put five dots, and so on.

Bumblies

Imperial/Metric
2 oz./50 g. butter
1 oz./25 g. castor sugar
3 oz./75 g. plain flour
currants
chocolate buttons

American
$\frac{1}{4}$ cup butter
2 tablespoons granulated sugar
$\frac{3}{4}$ cup all-purpose flour
currants
chocolate mint wafers

Put the butter in a bowl and soften with a wooden spoon, add the sugar and beat together for 1 minute; then add the flour and mix with the spoon, then by hand to make a dough. Flour the working surface and knead the dough until smooth, then roll out to about $\frac{1}{8}$ inch (3 mm.) in thickness and stamp out rounds with a 2-inch (5-cm.) plain cutter, or use a small glass. Lift with a palette knife on to a greased baking tray, mark with a knife and press on currants for eyes and a nose. Bake in a moderate oven for about 15 minutes or until the edges are just golden. Leave to cool for a few minutes then remove to a wire tray. Fix the chocolate buttons to the bumblies for feet by marking across the top of each button with a hot knife, and holding in position until set.
Cooking time about 15 minutes
Oven temperature 325°F., 160°C., Gas Mark 3

Chocolate crisp ice cream

This is just a bit different from the usual ice cream and jelly, though those are always favourites with our children.

Imperial/Metric
2 oz./50 g. cornflakes
4 oz./100 g. plain chocolate
1 oz./25 g. butter
1 tablespoon hot water
1 family block vanilla ice cream

American
2 cups cornflakes
$\frac{2}{3}$ cup semi-sweet chocolate pieces
2 tablespoons butter
1 tablespoon hot water
1 quart vanilla ice cream

Crush the cornflakes until fairly small but not crumbs. Melt the chocolate, butter and water together in a saucepan and add the cornflakes. Stir well and leave to cool. Cut the ice cream into thin slices and put a layer in the bottom of a plastic container about 6 by 4 inches (15 by 10 cm.). Put a third of the chocolate mixture on top and press down well. Repeat these layers until both are used up, finishing with a layer of ice cream. Press down really well with a wooden spoon and refreeze. The ice cream should not unfreeze too much during preparation, so work fairly fast. Scoop out into little dishes.
Illustrated on page 51

Smartie cakes

Imperial/Metric
1 2-egg chocolate basic sandwich cake mixture (see page 46)
1 recipe vanilla glacé icing (see page 49)
1 tube Smarties

American
1 2-egg chocolate basic sandwich cake batter (see page 46)
1 recipe vanilla glacé icing (see page 49)
1 package m & m's

Put a teaspoonful of cake mixture into paper sweet cases and cook in a moderately hot oven for about 10 minutes. Cool. Put a little icing on top of each and top with a Smartie.
Cooking time about 10 minutes.
Oven temperature 375°F., 190°C., Gas Mark 5

Corn crisps

Imperial/Metric
4 oz./100 g. plain chocolate
2 oz./50 g. margarine
1 tablespoon golden syrup
3 oz./75 g. cornflakes
2 oz./50 g. raisins

American
$\frac{2}{3}$ cup semi-sweet chocolate pieces
$\frac{1}{4}$ cup margarine
1 tablespoon corn syrup
3 cups cornflakes
$\frac{1}{3}$ cup raisins

Melt the chocolate in a basin over a pan of hot water. Melt the margarine, add the syrup, combine with the chocolate, stir in the cornflakes and raisins, mix well and put into paper cases.
Illustrated on page 51

Small meringues

Imperial/Metric
2 egg whites
4 oz./100 g. castor sugar
1 teaspoon vinegar (optional)

American
2 egg whites
$\frac{1}{2}$ cup granulated sugar
1 teaspoon vinegar (optional)

Beat the egg whites until stiff, add half the sugar and beat again until like marshmallow. Stir in the rest of the sugar and the vinegar if used. Pipe into tiny meringues on greaseproof paper which has been oiled and dry out in a very cool oven for several hours. If you like, you can colour half the mixture pink with a little cochineal. Arrange in a pyramid on a plate or sandwich pairs together with whipped cream. Meringues keep well in an airtight tin.
Cooking time several hours.
Oven temperature 225°F., 110°C., Gas Mark $\frac{1}{4}$

Suppers for two

The quick suppers in this section are for the evenings when you don't want to cook a full-scale meal but just want something to keep the wolf from the door. They can all be prepared in under 10 minutes, though some of them take longer to cook. All these recipes are made out of things you are likely to have in the cupboard or fridge, so you can make a last-minute decision to have them without rushing out to the shops.

The special suppers are for the times when there is a birthday or anniversary, you just feel like cooking something out of the ordinary, or you have to break the news about backing the car into a lamp post yet again. These recipes are mostly not suitable for large numbers since they either need last-minute attention or the ingredients are expensive. We suggest starting the meal with something very simple to prepare, fresh asparagus, prawns, smoked salmon or one of our own favourites given below; and do try the delicious puddings, for this is a time to indulge yourselves.

Quick supper ideas

Tuna and rice bake Make up a packet of savoury tomato rice. Drain and flake a can of tuna fish and stir into the rice. Heat gently and serve with grated cheese on top.

Cold tuna salad Drain and flake a can of tuna fish and mix with 3 tablespoons (scant ¼ cup) mayonnaise and plenty of fresh black pepper. Pile on to hot buttered toast and top with tomato slices.

Sardines, tomato and cheese on toast Drain a can of sardines and lay on hot buttered toast or fried bread. Put a little tomato purée on top and sprinkle liberally with grated cheese. Grill for 5 minutes until the cheese is melted and bubbling.

Grilled ham and cheese Lay a piece of ham on some buttered toast, top with sliced cheese and tomatoes. Season well and grill for a few minutes until hot.

Omelettes Fill with fried chicken livers and mushrooms.

Toasted bacon, lettuce and tomato sandwiches Use mayonnaise instead of butter as this prevents the toast going soggy.

Tuna Florentine Combine a large packet of frozen spinach, or 1 lb. (450 g.) freshly cooked spinach, with 2 tablespoons cream and put in the bottom of a casserole. Add a large can of tuna fish to ½ pint (3 dl., 1¼ cups) cheese sauce and heat together. Pour over the spinach and cover with grated cheese. Brown in the oven and serve with toast triangles round the edge and tomatoes.

Leeks and ham in cheese sauce Boil 4 leeks until just tender. Drain them well and wrap each in a slice of ham. Put on the base of a flat ovenproof dish and cover them with ½ pint (3 dl., 1¼ cups) cheese sauce. Sprinkle cheese over the top and put in a moderately hot oven for 20 minutes (375°F., 190°C., Gas Mark 5). You could use spinach or chicory instead of leeks if you like.

Frankfurters with sauerkraut

Imperial/Metric	American
1 can sauerkraut	**1 can sauerkraut**
2 rashers bacon	**2 slices bacon**
1 small apple	**1 small apple**
oil	**oil**
1 teaspoon caraway seeds (optional)	**1 teaspoon caraway seeds (optional)**
required number frankfurters, fresh or canned	**required number frankfurters, fresh or canned**

Drain the sauerkraut and rinse for 1 minute under the cold tap. Remove the rind from the bacon and chop. Peel and chop the apple. Put the bacon in a

Bacon plait (page 16) and sausage tart (page 17)

saucepan and fry with a little oil, add the apple, cook for 1 minute, then add the sauerkraut and caraway seeds. Stir well, put the frankfurters on top of this mixture and cook until they are hot. Serve with plenty of mustard and bread.

Cooking time few minutes

Quick pizza

Imperial/Metric	American
4 thick slices white bread	4 thick slices white bread
few slices cooked ham or bacon	few slices cooked ham or bacon
sliced tomato	sliced tomato
oregano	oregano
pepper	pepper
Bel Paese cheese or a Dutch cheese, thinly sliced	Bel Paese cheese or a Dutch cheese, thinly sliced
anchovy fillets	anchovy fillets
black olives	ripe olives

Grease a baking tray with margarine. Cut the crusts from the bread and put the slices of bread on the tray. Cover each slice with the ham or bacon and sliced tomato, sprinkle on a little oregano and pepper, cover with cheese and a few fillets of anchovy arranged in a lattice, plus a few black olives. Bake in a hot oven for 10 minutes.

Cooking time 10 minutes

Oven temperature 425°F., 220°C., Gas Mark 7

Hash

Imperial/Metric	American
2 medium-sized onions	2 medium-sized onions
butter	butter
2–3 boiled potatoes	2–3 boiled potatoes
1 small can corned beef	1 small can corned beef
salt and pepper	salt and pepper
eggs	eggs
Worcestershire sauce	Worcestershire sauce

Roughly chop the onions and cook until soft in butter. Dice the potatoes and add to the onions, fry for a few minutes; cut the corned beef into chunks and add, cook and stir until everything is well mixed and a little crisp. Fry the required number of eggs and serve on the hash. Add a little Worcestershire sauce and serve with some pickles.

Cooking time few minutes

Spanish baked eggs

This dish is made from the sort of ingredients you often find waiting patiently in their little cans, jars and polythene bags for a chance to be used up.

Imperial/Metric	American
1 onion	1 onion
1 clove garlic	1 clove garlic
oil	oil
3 tomatoes, fresh or canned	3 tomatoes, fresh or canned
salt and pepper	salt and pepper
pinch sugar	pinch sugar
2 tablespoons water	3 tablespoons water
few cooked peas, beans or mushrooms (optional)	few cooked peas, beans or mushrooms (optional)
little chopped ham or cooked bacon	little chopped ham or cooked bacon
4 eggs	4 eggs
1 red pimento (optional)	1 red pimiento (optional)

Chop the onion and garlic and fry in the oil until soft but not brown. Skin and chop the tomatoes and add to the pan, season and add the sugar and water. Cook very gently, covered, for 10 minutes, stir in the peas and half the ham or bacon. Divide the mixture into two small shallow heatproof dishes and break the eggs on to the vegetables. Cut the pimento into strips and garnish the eggs with this and the remaining ham or bacon. Cook in a hot oven for about 5 minutes so that the whites set quickly, leaving the yolks liquid. Serve with fresh bread.

Cooking time about 5 minutes

Oven temperature 425°F., 220°C., Gas Mark 7

Blender cheese soufflé

This can be made just as well with a can of flaked salmon or some chopped ham instead of the cheese.

Imperial/Metric	American
1½ oz./40 g. butter	3 tablespoons butter
½ pint/3 dl. milk	1¼ cups milk
1 thin slice white bread	1 thin slice white bread
½ teaspoon dry mustard	½ teaspoon dry mustard
½ teaspoon salt	½ teaspoon salt
pinch pepper	pinch pepper
4 oz./100 g. Cheddar cheese, diced	1 cup diced Cheddar cheese
4 eggs, separated	4 eggs, separated

Heat the butter and the milk together to melt the butter. Into the blender put the bread, mustard and salt and pepper. Gradually add the hot milk. Turn on for 1 minute. Add the cheese and blend for 10 seconds. Add the egg yolks and blend for a further 12 seconds.

Butter a 2-pint (1-litre, 5-cup) soufflé dish and beat the egg whites until stiff. Put them in the soufflé dish and fold in the cheese mixture with a metal spoon. Bake in a moderately hot oven for 35 minutes. If it is getting too brown lower the heat for the last 10 minutes. Serve immediately.

Cooking time 35 minutes
Oven temperature 375°F., 190°C., Gas Mark 5

Country omelette

An excellent way of putting leftovers to good use.

Imperial/Metric	American
2 onions	2 onions
oil	oil
2 medium-sized boiled potatoes (if raw fry with the onion)	2 medium-sized boiled potatoes (if raw fry with the onion)
1 clove garlic	1 clove garlic
2 rashers streaky bacon	2 slices bacon
any combination of the following: peas, cut green beans, carrots, cooked chicken or ham, green or red peppers, chopped salami or garlic sausage	any combination of the following: peas, cut green beans, carrots, cooked chicken or ham, green or red sweet peppers, chopped salami or garlic sausage
4 eggs	4 eggs
salt and pepper	salt and pepper

Roughly chop the onions and fry in a little oil; when soft add the chopped potatoes, chopped garlic, bacon, vegetables and meat. Heat thoroughly. If you like individual omelettes, remove half the mixture to a plate and make two separate omelettes. Lightly beat the eggs with salt and pepper, pour them over the contents of the frying pan and shake to distribute the egg. When the egg is set, hold a large plate over the pan, tip the pan over and slide the omelette back into the frying pan to cook the other side.

Cooking time few minutes

Special suppers
Stuffed avocados

Apart from the usual prawns, there are lots of things that go very well with avocados. If possible, prepare the avocados no more than 1 hour before eating as they discolour. A sprinkle of lemon juice will help to prevent this. Cut the avocado in half lengthways and remove the stone, then fill with any of the following:

Sour cream mixed with chopped chives, salt and pepper and a good spoonful of that cheap Danish caviar.

A small can of crabmeat mixed with a little lemon juice, mayonnaise and a very little cayenne pepper.

2 oz. (50 g., ½ cup) Danish Blue cheese mixed with 2 oz. (50 g.) cream cheese, a dash of Worcestershire sauce and a dash of Tabasco or cayenne pepper. If the mixture is too stiff, mix in a little mayonnaise.

Finely chopped celery, apple, pimento and hard-boiled egg in mayonnaise.

Kipper pâté (see page 71).

Simple chicken liver pâté

Imperial/Metric	American
8 oz./225 g. chicken livers	½ lb. chicken livers
2 oz./50 g. butter	¼ cup butter
2 oz./50 g. finely chopped onion	½ cup finely chopped onion
1 clove garlic, finely chopped	1 clove garlic, finely chopped
2 tablespoons brandy	3 tablespoons brandy
salt and pepper	salt and pepper

Wash the chicken livers and remove any pieces that have a greenish tinge. Melt the butter slowly, gently fry the onion and garlic and when soft add the chicken livers and cook for a few minutes; they must still be a little pink in the centre when you remove them from the heat. Put them in a blender with the brandy and seasoning if you like a very smooth pâté; you might need a little milk or more brandy to prevent it sticking. For a rougher texture just mash it all with a fork. Put it in a small dish, cover with a little melted butter if you like and chill. It is best made a day before it is needed. Eat with hot buttered toast.

Cooking time few minutes

Mushrooms in breadcrumbs

Imperial/Metric	American
8 oz./225 g. button mushrooms	2 cups button mushrooms
1 egg, beaten	1 egg, beaten
dried brown breadcrumbs	dried brown bread crumbs
oil or butter for frying	oil or butter for frying
1 lemon	1 lemon

Wash the mushrooms, but leave them whole with their stalks on. Trim them if you like. Dip them into the beaten egg and then into breadcrumbs. Fry them in hot butter or oil and drain on kitchen paper. Serve with wedges of lemon and thin brown bread and butter. They should be crisp on the outside, but tender inside.

Cooking time few minutes

Artichokes with ham

This takes just a couple of minutes but it is very good.

Imperial/Metric	American
1 can artichoke hearts	1 can artichoke hearts
1 good slice ham or 2 rashers bacon	1 good slice ham or 2 slices bacon
2 oz./50 g. butter	$\frac{1}{4}$ cup butter
chopped parsley	chopped parsley

Drain the artichokes and quarter them (1 can is more than enough for two). Chop the ham or bacon and fry gently for a few minutes in the butter, add the artichokes, heat thoroughly, then put into hot individual dishes with a little parsley on top. Serve with fresh bread to mop up the juice.

Cooking time few minutes

Prawn and mushroom salad

Imperial/Metric	American
4 oz./100 g. shelled prawns	$\frac{2}{3}$ cup shelled prawns or shrimp
4 oz./100 g. button mushrooms	1 cup button mushrooms
4 tablespoons French dressing	$\frac{1}{3}$ cup French dressing
juice of $\frac{1}{2}$ lemon	juice of $\frac{1}{2}$ lemon
few crisp lettuce leaves	few crisp lettuce leaves

Peel the prawns and slice the mushrooms thinly. Combine both with the French dressing and lemon juice and leave to stand for at least 1 hour. Pile on to crisp lettuce leaves and serve with thinly cut and buttered brown bread.

Lamb kebabs

Imperial/Metric	American
1 thick slice lamb taken from leg, about 12 oz./350 g.	1 thick slice lamb taken from leg, about $\frac{3}{4}$ lb.
some thick slices onion	some thick slices onion
4 oz./100 g. button mushrooms	1 cup button mushrooms
bay leaves	bay leaves
melted butter or oil	melted butter or oil
slices lemon	slices lemon
marinade	marinade
3 tablespoons oil	$\frac{1}{4}$ cup oil
1 tablespoon lemon juice	1 tablespoon lemon juice
1 onion, peeled and sliced	1 onion, peeled and sliced
1 clove garlic, peeled and chopped	1 clove garlic, peeled and chopped
pinch dried marjoram	pinch dried marjoram
salt and pepper	salt and pepper
1 tablespoon chopped parsley	1 tablespoon chopped parsley
1 small carrot, peeled and sliced	1 small carrot, peeled and sliced
cucumber and yogurt salad	cucumber and yogurt salad
$\frac{1}{2}$ cucumber	$\frac{1}{2}$ cucumber
1 clove garlic	1 clove garlic
$\frac{1}{2}$ pint yogurt	$1\frac{1}{4}$ cups yogurt
white pepper and salt	white pepper and salt
1 tablespoon finely chopped mint	1 tablespoon finely chopped mint

Trim the meat and cut into 1-inch ($2\frac{1}{2}$-cm.) cubes; mix together in a large bowl the ingredients for the marinade and put the meat in it for at least 3 hours, preferably longer. Thread the meat with slices of onion, mushrooms and bay leaves on long skewers, brush with melted butter or oil. Cook under a moderate grill for 15–20 minutes, turning several times. Serve on a bed of rice with slices of lemon.

Cucumber and yogurt salad is excellent with kebabs. Dice the cucumber and leave to drain for 30 minutes, crush the garlic, add to the yogurt with salt and pepper to taste and add the mint (in desperation you can use a little mint from a jar of mint sauce). Taste again, then add the cucumber. Decorate with a few whole mint leaves if you can.

Cooking time 15–20 minutes

Buffet party menu one (pages 73–5)

Kidneys turbigo

Imperial/Metric	American
12 baby onions	12 baby onions
4 oz./100 g. mushrooms	1 cup mushrooms
5 lamb's kidneys	5 lamb kidneys
2 oz./50 g. butter	$\frac{1}{4}$ cup butter
4 oz./100 g. chipolata sausages	$\frac{1}{4}$ lb. small pork sausages
2 teaspoons flour	2 teaspoons flour
1 teaspoon tomato purée	1 teaspoon tomato paste
1 tablespoon sherry	1 tablespoon sherry
$\frac{1}{4}$–$\frac{1}{2}$ pint/$1\frac{1}{2}$–3 dl. beef stock	$\frac{2}{3}$–$1\frac{1}{4}$ cups beef stock
salt and pepper	salt and pepper
bay leaf	bay leaf
chopped parsley	chopped parsley

Boil the onions for 3 minutes and drain them. Quarter the mushrooms. Skin the kidneys, remove the core from the middle with scissors or a sharp knife and cut in half lengthways. Melt the butter in a deep frying pan and fry the sausages until brown on all sides. Take them out and slice each into three. Add the kidneys, fry briskly until brown and add to the sausages. Fry the onions and mushrooms for 2–3 minutes and draw to one side of the pan. Stir in the flour, purée, sherry and stock and bring to the boil. Season with salt and pepper and add the sausages, kidneys and bay leaf. Cover and simmer for 20 minutes. Serve, sprinkled with parsley, with plain boiled rice.

Cooking time about 30 minutes

Italian beef olives

Imperial/Metric	American
1 small onion	1 small onion
oil	oil
1 small can tomatoes	1 small can tomatoes
1 clove garlic	1 clove garlic
1 tablespoon chopped parsley	1 tablespoon chopped parsley
salt and pepper	salt and pepper
2 oz./50 g. cheese, grated	$\frac{1}{2}$ cup grated cheese
2 beef olives, each about 4 oz./100 g.	2 beef olives, each about $\frac{1}{4}$ lb.
1 egg, beaten and seasoned	1 egg, beaten and seasoned
brown breadcrumbs	brown bread crumbs

Chop the onion, and fry gently in a little oil for 5 minutes. Do not let it brown. Add the can of tomatoes,

the crushed garlic, parsley and salt and pepper and bring to the boil. Simmer gently for 10 minutes, without a lid. Stir frequently. Add $1\frac{1}{2}$ oz. (40 g., 6 tablespoons) cheese and stir until melted. Keep warm.

Meanwhile beat the beef olives with a rolling pin between two pieces of wet greaseproof paper, until about twice their original size and quite thin. Dip them in the beaten egg, and then cover both sides in breadcrumbs. Fry in hot oil for 2 minutes on each side. Place them in the grill pan and cover the top with the tomato sauce. Sprinkle the remaining cheese on top. Brown under the grill, until the cheese is bubbling. Serve very hot with mashed potatoes and a green salad.

Cooking time about 25 minutes

Windsor chicken

Imperial/Metric	American
2 chicken breasts	2 chicken breasts
1 oz./25 g. butter	2 tablespoons butter
1 tablespoon chopped tarragon, fresh or dried	1 tablespoon chopped tarragon, fresh or dried
sauce	sauce
1 oz./25 g. butter	2 tablespoons butter
1 oz./25 g. flour	$\frac{1}{4}$ cup flour
$\frac{1}{4}$ pint/$1\frac{1}{2}$ dl. milk	$\frac{2}{3}$ cup milk
1 teaspoon French mustard	1 teaspoon French mustard
3 tablespoons dry white wine	$\frac{1}{4}$ cup dry white wine
salt, pepper, nutmeg	salt, pepper, nutmeg
2 oz./50 g. Swiss or Cheddar cheese, grated	$\frac{1}{2}$ cup grated Swiss or Cheddar cheese
2 slices ham	2 slices ham
dried breadcrumbs	dried bread crumbs

Wash and dry the chicken. Cream together the butter and tarragon and spread over the chicken. Put in a shallow ovenproof dish and cook in a moderately hot oven for 40–45 minutes or until tender, basting a few times. To make the sauce, melt the butter, stir in the flour, slowly add the milk, and bring to the boil stirring. Simmer for a few minutes, then add the mustard, wine and seasonings. Add the cheese, reserving a little, and stir until the cheese has melted. Remove the chicken from the oven and heat the grill. Put a slice of ham over each piece of chicken, pour over the sauce, sprinkle extra cheese and a few breadcrumbs on the top and grill until golden brown. Serve with new potatoes tossed in butter and French beans.

Cooking time about 50 minutes
Oven temperature 375°F., 190°C., Gas Mark 5

Fried pork fillet with lemon

Imperial/Metric	American
1 pork fillet	1 pork tenderloin
1 egg	1 egg
salt and pepper	salt and pepper
brown breadcrumbs for coating	brown bread crumbs for coating
2 oz./50 g. butter	¼ cup butter
1 tablespoon oil	1 tablespoon oil
juice of 1 lemon	juice of 1 lemon

Trim away any fat from the meat and cut into 2-inch (5-cm.) pennies. Put each slice between pieces of wetted greaseproof paper and beat until thin with a rolling pin. The paper stops the meat sticking to the rolling pin. Beat the egg with salt and pepper and dip the slices of meat first in the beaten egg and then in the breadcrumbs. Melt the butter and oil together in a frying pan, add the pieces of pork and fry gently for about 3 minutes on each side. Keep them hot in the oven on absorbent kitchen paper. Serve with the lemon juice squeezed over them and the juices from the pan. Scalloped potatoes (see page 25) go well with these and so do courgette slices fried in butter and sprinkled with garlic salt and pepper.
Cooking time about 6 minutes

Gougère

Imperial/Metric	American
1 recipe choux pastry (see page 47)	1 recipe choux paste (see page 47)
2 oz./50 g. Cheddar cheese, finely diced	½ cup finely diced Cheddar cheese
salt and pepper	salt and pepper
1 teaspoon made mustard	1 teaspoon made mustard
filling	filling
1 small onion	1 small onion
¾ oz./20 g. butter	1½ tablespoons butter
½ oz./15 g. flour	2 tablespoons flour
¼ pint/1½ dl. stock	⅔ cup stock
6 oz./175 g. diced cooked chicken	1 cup diced cooked chicken
2 oz./50 g. mushrooms, sliced and fried in a little butter	½ cup sliced mushrooms, fried in a little butter
1 teaspoon tomato ketchup or chutney	1 teaspoon tomato ketchup or chutney
salt and pepper	salt and pepper
1 oz./25 g. Cheddar cheese, grated	¼ cup grated Cheddar cheese
1 teaspoon chopped parsley	1 teaspoon chopped parsley

First prepare the choux pastry mixture as on page 47, stir in the cheese and season well with salt, pepper and mustard. Put on one side.

To make the filling, chop the onion and soften in the butter without colouring. Stir in the flour, add the stock and bring to the boil, stirring. Draw aside, add the chicken, mushrooms, ketchup and seasoning. Butter an oval ovenproof dish, about 10 inches (25 cm.) long, and spoon the cheese pastry mixture round the edge in a thick border. Turn the chicken filling into the centre and sprinkle the grated cheese over the whole dish. Bake in a moderately hot oven for about 35–40 minutes. Serve very hot, sprinkled with parsley, with potato crisps and a salad.
Cooking time 35–40 minutes
Oven temperature 400°F., 200°C., Gas Mark 6

Chinese pork chops

Imperial/Metric	American
1 tablespoon soy sauce	1 tablespoon soy sauce
2 tablespoons sherry	3 tablespoons sherry
1 teaspoon light brown sugar	1 teaspoon light brown sugar
1 clove garlic, crushed	1 clove garlic, crushed
2 large pork chops	2 large pork chops
oil	oil
1 oz./25 g. butter	2 tablespoons butter
1 large onion, sliced	1 large onion, sliced
4 carrots, cut in thin strips	4 carrots, cut in thin strips
1 tablespoon flour	1 tablespoon flour
½ pint/3 dl. chicken stock	1¼ cups chicken stock

In a cup mix together the soy sauce, sherry, sugar and garlic. Cut the rind off the chops and put them in a shallow dish. Pour the sherry sauce over and leave for 1 hour to marinate. Pour a little oil into the bottom of a lidded frying pan or casserole, drain the chops, keeping the sauce on one side, and fry the chops until brown. Take out the chops and put on one side. Wipe out the casserole, melt the butter in it and fry the onion for 1 minute. Add the carrots with the flour and stir well. Add the stock, and bring to the boil, stirring. Put the chops on top and pour the marinade sauce over. Cover the pan and cook in a moderate oven until tender, about 1 hour. Serve with creamy mashed potatoes.
Cooking time about 1 hour
Oven temperature 325°F., 160°C., Gas Mark 3

Individual liqueur soufflés

Imperial/Metric	American
3 eggs	3 eggs
2 tablespoons castor sugar	3 tablespoons granulated sugar
little grated orange rind	little grated orange rind
3 tablespoons liqueur of choice or rum	¼ cup liqueur of choice or rum

Grease individual soufflé dishes. Separate the eggs, beat the yolks with the sugar until light and creamy. Beat the whites until stiff, fold into the yolk mixture, add the orange rind and half the liqueur. Put in the dishes and bake in a hot oven for 8–10 minutes until well risen and golden; it's better to under- than overcook or they get tough. Before serving, sprinkle on a little more liqueur and sugar.

Cooking time 8–10 minutes
Oven temperature 425°F., 220°C., Gas Mark 7

Mango fool

As a change from the more mundane fruits, try this, it is delicious.

Imperial/Metric	American
1 can mangos	1 can mangos
¼ pint/1½ dl. double cream	⅔ cup whipping cream
little coffee sugar or demerara	little brown sugar

Drain the fruit and put in a blender with the cream; blend until smooth and thick. Pour into glasses (it really makes three so save one). Chill for a few hours then sprinkle with sugar before serving.

Cointreau ice cream

Imperial/Metric	American
½ pint/3 dl. double cream	1¼ cups heavy cream
juice of ½ lemon	juice of ½ lemon
2 oz./50 g. castor sugar	¼ cup granulated sugar
3–4 tablespoons Cointreau or any other liqueur	¼–⅓ cup Cointreau or any other liqueur

Beat all the ingredients together until fairly stiff and pile into individual glass dishes. Freeze in the ice compartment of the fridge for 2–4 hours and serve with fan wafers.

Freezing time 2–4 hours

Banana flambé

This must be the best way of eating bananas. Experiment to find exactly how much lemon juice you like and try them with brandy or Grand Marnier.

Imperial/Metric	American
2 oz./50 g. butter	¼ cup butter
4 bananas	4 bananas
2 tablespoons soft brown sugar	3 tablespoons soft brown sugar
rind and juice of 1 medium orange	rind and juice of 1 medium orange
juice of ½ lemon	juice of ½ lemon
little rum	little rum

Assemble the ingredients before sitting down to dinner, then it takes just a few minutes to cook the bananas. Melt the butter in a frying pan, peel the bananas. Add the sugar, orange rind and juice with the lemon juice (more or less according to taste) to the pan, cook gently for a few minutes, then add the whole bananas. Cook gently, turning once and spooning the sauce over the bananas; after a few minutes add 2 tablespoons rum. When the bananas are soft but not sloppy, light a match then pour a little more rum into the pan, light and serve.

Cooking time few minutes

White peaches with almonds

Imperial/Metric	American
1 can white peach halves or pears	1 can white peach halves or pears
2 oz./50 g. ground almonds	½ cup ground almonds
1 oz./25 g. castor sugar	2 tablespoons granulated sugar
1 oz./25 g. softened butter	2 tablespoons softened butter

Drain the peaches and put cut side uppermost in a baking dish. Pour a little of the juice into the bottom of the dish. Mix the almonds, sugar and butter together to make a paste and press a ball of this mixture into the centre of each peach half. Bake in a moderate oven for about 20 minutes. Serve with double cream.

Cooking time about 20 minutes
Oven temperature 350°F., 180°C., Gas Mark 4

Variation
Use a can of ordinary peaches. Put them in the dish and sprinkle with 2 tablespoons brown sugar mixed with 1 teaspoon cinnamon and 1 teaspoon mixed spice. Bake as above and serve with cream and almond wafers (see page 69).

Social demands

Whether you are having the family for Sunday lunch, some friends for supper or a much owed party for 24, the first thing is not to panic and think you can't do it. Entertaining can be very easy, but this is the one time that a little organisation really pays off. Always prepare as much as possible the day before. In this section on dinner parties all the recipes can be prepared either the day before or, if not, in the morning. The ingredients have been carefully selected in that they can be obtained in all towns and throughout the year.

We have also tried to make each menu not too expensive, and if one course is a bit costly, the others are then definitely not. In order to help you we have given complete menus.

Each dish has maximum effect for minimum effort – the secret of this book! There is no need to feel that you must produce a banquet every time you entertain. The time will come when you are free to spend the whole day without interruption, preparing some fantastic pastry – but this is not it. Just take things calmly and you will find all goes well. One important thing to remember is to be ready yourself. Nobody minds waiting half an hour for the food to finish cooking – but it looks rather bad if you are seen disappearing upstairs in your apron just as the guests arrive. It makes them feel they've arrived too early, and are therefore slightly unwelcome. So above all keep your head, and outwardly anyway appear to be in command of the situation.

Each menu serves six people.

Menu one **Avocado and tomato salad**

Imperial/Metric	American
dressing	dressing
4 tablespoons oil	**⅓ cup oil**
1 tablespoon wine vinegar	**1 tablespoon wine vinegar**
1 tablespoon lemon juice	**1 tablespoon lemon juice**
½ teaspoon mustard	**½ teaspoon mustard**
½ teaspoon sugar	**¼ teaspoon sugar**
salt and pepper	**salt and pepper**
salad	salad
2 large avocados, peeled and sliced	**2 large avocados, peeled and sliced**
4 large tomatoes, peeled and sliced	**4 large tomatoes, peeled and sliced**
1 onion, cut into very thin rings	**1 onion, cut into very thin rings**
1 tablespoon parsley	**1 tablespoon parsley**

First make the dressing by putting all the ingredients into a screw-top jar and shaking well for 1 minute. Put the avocados and tomatoes into a serving dish with the onion rings arranged on top. Sprinkle with parsley and pour the dressing over. Leave to stand in the fridge for at least 1 hour before serving. Serve with granary bread and butter.

Hungarian goulash

Imperial/Metric	American
1½ lb./675 g. chuck steak	1½ lb. chuck steak
2 tablespoons dripping or oil	3 tablespoons drippings or oil
2 medium-sized onions, sliced	2 medium-sized onions, sliced
1 tablespoon paprika	1 tablespoon paprika
1 tablespoon flour	1 tablespoon flour
2 teaspoons tomato purée	2 teaspoons tomato paste
¾–1 pint/4–6 dl. beef stock made with 1 stock cube and water	2–2½ cups beef stock made with 1 bouillon cube and water
1 bouquet garni	1 bouquet garni
1 clove garlic, crushed	1 clove garlic, crushed
salt and pepper	salt and pepper
2 red peppers, seeded and sliced, or 1 small can	2 sweet red peppers, seeded and sliced, or 1 small can
3 tomatoes, peeled and sliced	3 tomatoes, peeled and sliced
¼ pint/1½ dl. sour cream	⅔ cup sour cream

Cut the meat into squares, brown quickly in the hot dripping and take out. Lower the heat and add the sliced onions and after a few minutes the paprika. Cook slowly for 1 minute, then add the flour, purée and stock. Stir until boiling, replace the meat, add the bouquet garni, garlic and seasoning. Simmer gently on the stove top or in a moderate oven for about 2 hours or until the meat is tender. Just before serving, add the sliced peppers and tomatoes and serve immediately. Serve with the sour cream and noodles and a salad.

Cooking time about 2 hours

Oven temperature 325°F., 160°C., Gas Mark 3

Iced coffee soufflés

Imperial/Metric	American
4 eggs	4 eggs
4 oz./100 g. castor sugar	½ cup granulated sugar
2 tablespoons powdered coffee, or granules dissolved with 1 tablespoon hot water	3 tablespoons powdered coffee, or granules dissolved with 1 tablespoon hot water
2 oz./50 g. plain chocolate	⅓ cup semi-sweet chocolate pieces
2 tablespoons water	3 tablespoons water
2 tablespoons rum or brandy	3 tablespoons rum or brandy
7 fl. oz./2 dl. double cream	scant cup heavy cream
2 oz./50 g. grated chocolate	⅓ cup grated semi-sweet chocolate

Separate the eggs and beat the yolks with the sugar and coffee until the mixture is thick and creamy. Melt the chocolate and water in a small bowl over hot water, add the rum or brandy and beat into the egg and coffee mixture. Whip the cream and fold into the mixture. Whisk the egg whites until stiff and fold into the mixture, fold in the grated chocolate and spoon into individual soufflé dishes. Freeze for at least 4 hours. If using the day they are made, save a little of the cream for decoration and sprinkle on a little extra grated chocolate.

Freezing time 4 hours

Menu two **Melon with ginger**

A very simple refreshing start to a deliciously rich meal. Frozen melon balls could be used at a pinch.

Imperial/Metric	American
1 melon, honeydew or whatever is available	1 melon, honeydew or whatever is available
2 pieces stem ginger plus syrup	2 pieces preserved ginger plus syrup
few mint leaves	few mint leaves

Cut the ripe melon flesh into small cubes or make melon balls if you have the right gadget; put in a large bowl. Cut the stem ginger into very small pieces, add to the melon with 2 tablespoons ginger syrup and leave in the fridge for 1 hour. Cover the bowl or everything in the fridge will taste of ginger. Spoon into individual glasses and decorate with a few mint leaves. Use more ginger if liked.

Stuffed pork fillet

Imperial/Metric	American
2 pork fillets, about 12 oz./350 g. each	2 pork tenderloins, about ¾ lb. each
3 large Spanish onions	3 large Spanish onions
1 head celery	1 bunch celery
1 oz./25 g. butter	2 tablespoons butter
¼ pint/1½ dl. chicken stock	⅔ cup chicken stock
salt and pepper	salt and pepper
1 small carton cream	1 small carton cream
stuffing	**stuffing**
1 medium-sized onion, finely chopped	1 medium-sized onion, finely chopped
1 oz./25 g. butter	2 tablespoons butter
6 oz./175 g. minced pork	¾ cup ground pork
2 oz./50 g. fresh breadcrumbs	1 cup fresh bread crumbs
2 teaspoons fresh or dried sage, chopped	2 teaspoons fresh or dried sage, chopped
2 teaspoons chopped parsley	2 teaspoons chopped parsley
salt and pepper	salt and pepper
1 egg	1 egg

First make the stuffing. Soften the onion in the butter without colouring and put into a bowl with the minced pork, breadcrumbs, sage, parsley and seasoning. Mix well and bind with the egg.

Remove any skin from the fillets and split them down the centre to open them out. Lay each between two pieces of greaseproof paper and beat them slightly to flatten them. Spread the stuffing on one, then cover with the other, arranging them head to tail. Roll them slightly to neaten the shape, then sew up or tie them with string. Slice the onions and celery. Heat the butter in a flameproof casserole and brown the pork on both sides. Take out, put in the onion and celery, and cook for about 5 minutes, stirring fairly frequently. Put the pork on top and pour in the stock. Season, cover tightly, and cook in a moderate oven for about 45 minutes. Take out the pork, lift out the onion and celery with a draining spoon and arrange on a serving dish. Remove the string from the pork, slice it and arrange on the top of the vegetables. Adjust the seasoning of the gravy, boil up and add the cream. Continue to boil until like syrup for about 2 minutes and then spoon over the dish.

Cooking time about 1 hour
Oven temperature 325°F., 160°C., Gas Mark 3

Raspberry brûlée

This should be prepared the day before.

Imperial/Metric	American
about 1 lb./450 g. fresh or frozen raspberries, or 2 cans	about 3 cups fresh or frozen raspberries, or 2 cans
½ pint/3 dl. double cream	1¼ cups whipping cream
2 oz./50 g. demerara sugar	¼ cup brown sugar, firmly packed

Put the fruit in a shallow ovenproof dish. If using canned fruit, drain off most of the juice. Whip the cream and spread over the fruit. Put the sugar on the fruit and leave the dish in the fridge until required. Heat the grill until hot, then put the pudding under the grill until the sugar melts. Serve immediately, with almond wafers.

Almond wafers

Imperial/Metric	American
2 oz./50 g. butter	¼ cup butter
2 oz./50 g. castor sugar	¼ cup granulated sugar
2 oz./50 g. ground almonds	½ cup ground almonds
2 teaspoons flour	2 teaspoons flour
1 tablespoon milk	1 tablespoon milk

Grease the baking sheets. Put in a small saucepan the butter, sugar and almonds; melt slowly, stir well, then remove from the heat, add the flour and milk and beat thoroughly. Put teaspoonfuls of the mixture on the tray, well apart, and cook in a moderately hot oven for 6–8 minutes. Grease a rolling pin. Remove the biscuits from the oven and leave to cool for 1 minute, then lift with a palette knife on to the rolling pin and leave to set. If the mixture hardens too quickly, before you have finished rolling the biscuits, put the tray back in the oven for 1 minute to soften the mixture. Store in an airtight tin.

Cooking time 6–8 minutes
Oven temperature 375°F., 190°C., Gas Mark 5

Menu three Potato and watercress soup

Imperial/Metric	American
1 onion	1 onion
1½ oz./40 g. butter	3 tablespoons butter
3 large potatoes	3 large potatoes
1¾ pints/1 litre chicken stock	4½ cups chicken stock
seasoning	seasoning
1 bunch watercress	1 bunch watercress
¼ pint milk/1½ dl. milk or single cream	⅔ cup milk or coffee cream
croûtons	croûtons

Peel and chop the onion and cook in the melted butter until transparent. Peel the potatoes and cut them into thick slices. Add them to the pan and cook for 2–3 minutes. Pour in the stock, season, bring to the boil and simmer, covered, until the potato is tender, about 20 minutes. Five minutes before the end of the cooking time add the watercress. Liquidise in an electric blender until creamy. You can put it through a sieve, but it takes rather longer. Return to the saucepan and add the milk or cream. Do not boil or it may curdle. Serve with fried croûtons, made with tiny squares of bread, fried until crisp in a mixture of oil and butter.
Cooking time 30 minutes

Dutch meatballs

Imperial/Metric	American
1 lb./450 g. chuck steak	1 lb. chuck steak
1 lb./450 g. minced pork	1 lb. ground pork
3 thick slices white bread	3 thick slices white bread
little milk	little milk
2 medium-sized onions	2 medium-sized onions
2 eggs	2 eggs
salt and pepper	salt and pepper
flour	flour
oil	oil
3 tablespoons tomato purée	¼ cup tomato paste
1 beef stock cube	1 beef bouillon cube
1 pint/6 dl. water	2½ cups water
about 12 black olives	about 12 black olives
¼ pint/1½ dl. sour cream	⅔ cup sour cream

Mince the meats twice. Remove the crusts from the bread, break in pieces, pour over a little milk and leave to soak. Peel and roughly chop the onions. Put the eggs, onion, salt and pepper in the blender and blend thoroughly. Combine with the meat and bread and beat well. Roll the mixture into walnut-sized balls. Roll the meatballs in flour. Heat the oil in a large frying pan and fry the meatballs until brown, drain on paper and put them in a large casserole or saucepan. Add the purée to the pan drippings, add the crumbled stock cube and slowly add the water. Bring to the boil, simmer for a few minutes, season, then pour over the meatballs. Leave for at least 3 hours, they are best made in the morning. Reheat in the oven or with gentle direct heat, cook for a further 10 minutes. Then add the olives, gently stir in the sour cream (or serve sour cream separately) and heat for a few more minutes, but do not let the liquid boil. Serve with buttered egg noodles or plain rice and a mixed green salad.
Cooking time about 30 minutes

Apple and orange praline

Imperial/Metric	American
2 lb./900 g. cooking apples	2 lb. cooking apples
3 oz./75 g. sugar	6 tablespoons sugar
4 tablespoons water	⅓ cup water
1 oz./25 g. butter	2 tablespoons butter
grated rind of 1 orange	grated rind of 1 orange
3 tablespoons brandy	¼ cup brandy
3 seedless oranges	3 seedless oranges
praline	praline
2 tablespoons water	3 tablespoons water
3 oz./75 g. sugar	6 tablespoons sugar
2 oz./50 g. flaked almonds	½ cup flaked almonds

Peel and slice the apples and put in a heavy saucepan with the sugar and water; cook very gently, stirring from time to time. When the apples are soft, add the butter, orange rind and brandy. Cook until the sauce is thick. Leave to cool. Put the apple sauce in a glass dish. Peel the oranges, removing all the pith, and slice thinly into rings. Arrange in circles over the apples.

To make the praline, butter a baking tray. Boil the water and sugar in a small saucepan until the sugar caramelises and is golden brown. Stir in the almonds and bring back to the boil, then pour on to the buttered baking tray. Leave to cool. Break up with a rolling pin, but do not reduce it to a powder. Sprinkle over the oranges.
Cooking time 10–15 minutes

Menu four Kipper pâté

This can be made two days before and kept in the fridge. It also freezes very well.

Imperial/Metric	American
1 8-oz./227-g. packet kipper fillets	½ lb. kippered herring, boned
6 oz./175 g. Philadelphia cream cheese	¾ cup Philadelphia cream cheese
paprika and black pepper	paprika and black pepper
2–3 tablespoons top of the milk	3–4 tablespoons half and half

Cook the kippers for 15 minutes, scrape the skin off the back and mash them with a fork. There is no need to take out any bones unless you see a particularly large one. Put into the blender with the cheese, a large pinch of paprika and some black pepper and the top of the milk. Blend together until really smooth and pour into a small serving pot. It will thicken up in the fridge. Chill well and serve with hot toast and butter.

Chicken Suzanne

Imperial/Metric	American
6 chicken pieces	6 chicken pieces
seasoned flour	seasoned flour
3 tablespoons oil	¼ cup oil
3 oz./75 g. butter	6 tablespoons butter
¾ pint/4 dl. chicken stock	2 cups chicken stock
1 large orange	1 large orange
2 tablespoons lemon juice	3 tablespoons lemon juice
1½ oz./40 g. flour	6 tablespoons flour
salt and white pepper	salt and white pepper
6 oz./175 g. white grapes	1¼ cups green grapes
1 small orange (optional)	1 small orange (optional)

Wash and dry the chicken, put the seasoned flour in a bag and shake the chicken pieces one at a time in the flour. Put the oil and 1 oz. (25 g., 2 tablespoons) of the butter in a large saucepan and fry the chicken pieces a few at a time, until golden. Remove from the pan, pour off the fat and wipe out the pan with absorbent paper. Return the chicken to pan, add the chicken stock, juice and grated rind of the orange and lemon juice. Bring to the boil and simmer until the chicken is tender, about 35–45 minutes. Remove the chicken to a serving dish, put the flour in a small bowl with the remaining butter, and cream together; remove the pan from the heat and add the flour and butter in small pieces, stirring well. Return the pan to the heat, bring to the boil stirring and simmer for 1 minute. Peel and de-pip the grapes, add to the sauce and pour over the chicken. Garnish if liked with orange slices or wedges. Serve with creamy mashed potatoes and green beans and almonds.
Cooking time about 1 hour

Strawberry trifle

This is delicious, and only takes 5 minutes to make.

Imperial/Metric	American
2 jam Swiss rolls	2 jelly rolls
2 15-oz./425-g. cans strawberries	2 15-oz. cans strawberries
1 wine glass sherry	1 wine glass sherry
½ pint/3 dl. double cream	1¼ cups whipping cream

Cut each of the Swiss rolls into six slices and put the pieces in the bottom of a deep glass dish. Add the juice from one of the tins of strawberries and the sherry and mash with a fork until well mixed. Put the drained strawberries on top and cover with a thick layer of whipped cream. Chill for at least 1 hour before serving.

Menu five Hot anchovy and garlic dip

We suggest this unusual start to the meal as it can be eaten with a pre-dinner drink.

Imperial/Metric	American
vegetables, see method	vegetables, see method
1 can anchovies	1 can anchovies
2 small cloves garlic	2 small cloves garlic
12 fl. oz./3½ dl. double cream	1½ cups whipping cream
2 oz./50 g. butter	¼ cup butter
1 packet Italian bread sticks	1 package Italian bread sticks

Prepare a selection from the following vegetables. Wash and cut into lengths about 2 inches (5 cm.) long and ½ inch (1 cm.) thick: cucumber, green peppers, celery and carrots; cut mushrooms in half or quarters; prepare cauliflower sprigs, tomatoes in quarters and whole radishes and spring onions.

Put the prepared vegetables, not tomatoes or mushrooms, in a bowl of cold water with some ice cubes and leave in the fridge for 1 hour. Drain very well and arrange on a large flat plate or dish, cover with plastic wrap and put back in the fridge. To make the dip, drain the anchovies and chop; finely chop the garlic. Put the cream in a heavy saucepan and heat until boiling; cook for 15 minutes, stirring frequently. Melt the butter in a small saucepan, add the anchovies and garlic. Leave everything until required, then gently heat the anchovies, pour on the cream and heat gently, stirring. Transfer to a flameproof casserole or dish. Keep the dip warm by using an electric hot plate, spirit lamp or candle warmer. Serve accompanied by the vegetables and bread sticks. If the dip separates beat for 1 minute.

Cooking time about 20 minutes

Devilled chicken with turmeric rice

Imperial/Metric	American
6 chicken pieces	**6 chicken pieces**
1 teaspoon each ginger, mustard, curry powder, black pepper	**1 teaspoon each ginger, mustard, curry powder, black pepper**
3 teaspoons salt	**1 tablespoon salt**
oil	oil
3 tablespoons ketchup	**4 tablespoons ketchup**
2 tablespoons Worcestershire sauce	**3 tablespoons Worcestershire sauce**
2 tablespoons O.K. sauce	**3 tablespoons chutney or barbecue sauce**
2 tablespoons soy sauce	**3 tablespoons soy sauce**
½ pint chicken stock made with 1 stock cube and water	**1¼ cups chicken stock made with 1 bouillon cube and water**
cayenne pepper (optional)	cayenne pepper (optional)
turmeric rice	turmeric rice
10 oz./275 g. long-grain rice	**1½ cups long-grain rice**
2 oz./50 g. butter	**¼ cup butter**
1 medium-sized onion	**1 medium-sized onion**
1 teaspoon turmeric	**1 teaspoon turmeric**
3 tablespoons currants	**¼ cup currants**
salt and pepper	**salt and pepper**

The first part can be done a few hours before required. Wash and dry the chicken and mix together the ginger, mustard, curry powder, pepper and salt, rub well into the chicken and leave for 1–2 hours. Rub a little oil into the chicken on both sides, and grill for 10 minutes on each side, or until the skin is crisp and golden brown. Mix together the ketchup and sauces in a small bowl. Make up the stock and add to the sauces. If you like hot food add a little cayenne pepper to the sauce. Put the chicken in a large shallow dish or roasting tin and pour the sauce over. Cover the dish with foil until needed, then cook in a moderate oven, still covered, for 20 minutes, baste, and continue cooking uncovered for another 15 minutes or until the chicken is tender. Put on a serving dish with the sauce poured over and garnish with watercress. Serve with turmeric rice.

To make the turmeric rice, put the rice to cook in plenty of boiling salted water. Melt the butter, finely slice the onion, fry until golden, stir in the turmeric, fry for 1 minute, then add the well drained cooked rice and the currants. Stir well, season with salt and pepper and pile around the chicken. Serve with a green salad.

You can safely keep the chicken warm in the oven, but the longer it is left with the sauce the stronger the flavour will be.

Cooking time about 1 hour
Oven temperature 350°F., 180°C., Gas Mark 4

Sour cream cheese pie

Imperial/Metric	American
4 oz./100 g. digestive biscuit crumbs	**1 cup graham cracker crumbs**
2 oz./50 g. melted butter or margarine	**¼ cup melted butter or margarine**
8 oz./225 g. curd cheese or cream cheese	**1 cup curd cheese or cream cheese**
¼ pint/1½ dl. sour cream	**⅔ cup soured cream**
2 oz./50 g. sugar	**¼ cup sugar**
few drops vanilla essence	**few drops vanilla extract**
juice of 1 lemon	**juice of 1 lemon**
1 egg, beaten	**1 egg, beaten**
1 tablespoon flour	**1 tablespoon flour**

Mix the crumbs with the melted butter and smooth over the bottom of a cake tin with a loose base. Mix all the other ingredients together and beat well until smooth. Pour into the tin and bake in a moderate oven for 20 minutes. Cool and chill well before removing carefully from the tin. Serve on the base. It is much nicer if you make it the day before, and it freezes very well.

Cooking time 20 minutes
Oven temperature 350°F., 180°C., Gas Mark 4

Buffet parties

Here are two menus for cold buffet parties. The first is made up of cold dishes and would be particularly suitable for the summer, while the second combines both hot and cold dishes; but if you particularly like to serve a hot main course we suggest using double quantities of either Dutch meatballs or Hungarian goulash, which are in the previous section, as these can be eaten with a fork. Salads and vegetables should be in fork-sized pieces also. Serve with either baked potatoes in their jackets or noodles which can be cooked in advance and left in a bowl of cold water until you need them. To reheat noodles, drain well and cover with boiling water, bring to the boil and drain again, stirring in a knob of butter. It's not necessary to make all the quiches and salads given in the second menu; one or two would be enough with the chicken pie. When planning your party, prepare as much as possible the day before or at least in the morning. You can of course freeze all the dishes apart from the salads, and these can be left washed in plastic boxes or bags in the fridge for a couple of days. French dressing and mayonnaise both keep well too. Arrange the table and the flowers in the morning, and wrap sets of knives and forks in paper napkins. Put all the plates, dishes and coffee cups ready too. Make the dishes of food look as pretty as possible, using plenty of parsley and watercress to garnish. Serve a good selection of cheeses and biscuits and a bowl of fresh fruit with the puddings, and of course, plenty of fresh hot coffee. Both menus serve twelve people but you can easily double quantities to serve more.

Menu one Fish pâté

Imperial/Metric	American
1 7½-oz./213-g. can salmon	1 7½-oz. can salmon
1 7-oz./198-g. can tuna	1 7-oz. can tuna
1 3½-oz./99-g. can shrimps or 4 oz./100 g. peeled cooked prawns	1 3½-oz. can shrimp or ⅔ cup peeled cooked prawns or shrimp
6 oz./175 g. fresh white breadcrumbs	3 cups fresh white bread crumbs
4 oz./100 g. butter, melted	½ cup melted butter
2 lemons	2 lemons
3 teaspoons anchovy essence	3 teaspoons anchovy paste
¼ pint/1½ dl. single cream	⅔ cup coffee cream
salt and pepper	salt and pepper
little milk	little milk

Empty the contents of the cans of tuna and salmon into a bowl and flake the fish. Add the roughly chopped shrimps or prawns. Combine the breadcrumbs with the melted butter and grated rind and juice of the lemons. Mix with the fish and add the anchovy essence and the cream, season, and add sufficient milk to get the pâté to the required consistency. Divide into 12 individual soufflé dishes or leave until ready to serve, then place a portion on each plate with a wedge of lemon and toast. This is best made in the morning and left in the fridge.
Illustrated on page 63

French country pâté

Imperial/Metric	American
12 oz./350 g. pig's liver	¾ lb. pork liver
1 onion	1 onion
1 carrot	1 carrot
½ teaspoon dried thyme	½ teaspoon dried thyme
bay leaf	bay leaf
salt and pepper	salt and pepper
1 clove garlic, crushed	1 clove garlic, crushed
2 teaspoons chopped parsley	2 teaspoons chopped parsley
2 teaspoons wine vinegar	2 teaspoons wine vinegar
1 glass dry sherry	1 glass dry sherry
2 tablespoons oil	3 tablespoons oil
8 oz./225 g. sausage meat	1 cup sausage meat
4 oz./100 g. fatty bacon	5 slices bacon

Put the liver in a dish. Chop the onion and carrot finely and sprinkle over the liver. Add the thyme, bay leaf, salt and pepper, garlic and parsley. Put the vinegar and sherry over the top and sprinkle with the oil to make a film. Leave overnight or for several hours. Mince the liver and vegetables and add the sausage meat. Mix together with your hands and make sure no lumps of sausage meat are left. I'm afraid this is the best way to do it! Line a dish or loaf tin with the bacon rolled thin with a rolling pin and pour in the meat mixture. Cover and seal well with foil. Put in the middle of a moderate oven in a roasting tin one-third full of water and cook for 1½ hours. Spear with a skewer and if the juice which comes out is clear or very pale pink it's done. Empty the water away, cover with greaseproof paper and tie weights such as cans of fruit, etc., on top to press it. Leave until cold; serve sliced, with toast and butter or crisp French bread.
Cooking time 1½ hours
Oven temperature 350°F., 180°C., Gas Mark 4
Illustrated on page 63

Chicken in curried mayonnaise

Imperial/Metric	American
2 4-lb./1¾-kg. chickens, roasted or boiled	2 4-lb. chickens, roasted or boiled
sauce	sauce
1 tablespoon oil	1 tablespoon oil
3 oz./75 g. finely chopped onion	¾ cup finely chopped onion
2 teaspoons curry powder	2 teaspoons curry powder
2 teaspoons tomato purée	2 teaspoons tomato paste
1 wine glass red wine or sherry	1 wine glass red wine or sherry
1 wine glass water	1 wine glass water
bay leaf	bay leaf
salt, pepper and sugar	salt, pepper and sugar
3 slices lemon	3 slices lemon
juice of ½ lemon	juice of ½ lemon
¾ pint/4 dl. good mayonnaise	scant 2 cups good mayonnaise
2 teaspoons apricot jam	2 teaspoons apricot jam
more lemon juice if necessary	more lemon juice if necessary
3 tablespoons lightly whipped cream	¼ cup lightly whipped cream
little paprika	little paprika

To make the sauce, heat the oil, add the onion and cook slowly for 3–4 minutes. Add the curry powder and cook for another 1–2 minutes. Add the tomato purée, wine or sherry, water and bay leaf and bring to the boil. Add salt, pepper and sugar to taste, the lemon slices and the juice and simmer without a lid for 5–10 minutes. Strain and cool. Add gradually to the mayonnaise and then add the jam. Adjust seasoning and add more lemon juice if necessary. Add the cream. Cut up the chickens into pieces, removing the skin and bones, put on to a serving dish and coat with the sauce. Sprinkle with a little paprika.
Cooking time 10–15 minutes
Illustrated on page 63

Sweet pepper dressing

Imperial/Metric	American
½ pint/3 dl. oil	1¼ cups oil
¼ pint/1½ dl. wine vinegar	⅔ cup wine vinegar
1 teaspoon salt	1 teaspoon salt
1 teaspoon mustard	1 teaspoon mustard
2 teaspoons castor sugar	2 teaspoons granulated sugar
pepper to taste	pepper to taste
1 7-oz./198-g. can sweet red peppers, drained and chopped	1 7-oz. can sweet red peppers, drained and chopped

Place all the ingredients in a screw-top jar and shake hard until well mixed, chill well. It is better made the day before to allow the flavours to mix well.

Sunflower tomatoes

Imperial/Metric	American
12 button mushrooms	12 button mushrooms
sweet pepper dressing (see left)	sweet pepper dressing (see left)
12 large firm tomatoes	12 large firm tomatoes
1 curly endive or crisp lettuce	1 head chicory or crisp lettuce
salt and pepper	salt and pepper

Take the stalks off the mushrooms and put them in the sweet pepper dressing to marinate overnight. Cut each tomato into six segments, taking care not to slice right through to the base, and open out carefully like a flower. Put each tomato on a bed of endive or lettuce leaves and season with salt and pepper. Sit a mushroom in the centre of each of the tomatoes, reserving the marinade for the next recipe. Alternatively, simply serve van Dyked tomatoes as in the picture on page 63.

Sweet pepper rice

Imperial/Metric	American
1½ lb./675 g. long-grain rice	3½ cups long-grain rice
salted water	salted water
sweet pepper dressing (see above)	sweet pepper dressing (see above)
chopped parsley	chopped parsley

Boil the rice as usual for 12 minutes until just tender. Drain well and run under the hot tap to wash off the starch. Leave to cool. Fold the dressing (which you used to marinate the mushrooms in for the preceding recipe) through the rice, sprinkle with plenty of parsley and serve in a pretty dish.
Illustrated on page 63

Lemon sorbet

Imperial/Metric	American
1½ pints/scant litre water	3¾ cups water
6 oz./175 g. sugar	¾ cup sugar
finely grated rind and juice of 3 lemons	finely grated rind and juice of 3 lemons
2 egg whites	2 egg whites

Put the water and sugar into a saucepan and stir until dissolved over a low heat. Add the lemon rind, bring to the boil and boil rapidly for 5 minutes. Take off the heat and strain into a bowl. Add the lemon juice and cool. When the syrup is cold, beat the egg whites until stiff and stir them in. Pour into two large ice trays or plastic boxes and freeze until just hard, about 2 hours. Spoon the frozen mixture back into the bowl and whisk with a beater until it goes white and creamy. This whiteness comes from the air whisked into the mixture. Spoon back into the containers and freeze until ready to serve.
Freezing time minimum of 4 hours
Illustrated on page 63

Variation
Blackberry sorbet Cook 1 lb. (450 g.) blackberries in 2 tablespoons water with 2 oz. (50 g., ¼ cup) sugar. Blend, sieve and cool. Fold in egg whites and freeze.

Blackberry and pear gâteau

Imperial/Metric	American
meringue	meringue
5 egg whites	5 egg whites
5 oz./150 g. each castor and granulated sugar	1¼ cups fine granulated sugar
filling	filling
1 lb./450 g. blackberries	3 cups blackberries
2–4 oz./50–100 g. sugar	¼–½ cup sugar
3 pears or 1 can pears	3 pears or 1 can pears
1–2 teaspoons cornflour	1–2 teaspoons cornstarch
½ pint/3 dl. cream	1¼ cups cream

To make the meringue mixture, beat the egg whites until stiff, beat in the castor sugar and then fold in the granulated sugar. Put three-quarters of the meringue into a piping bag with a plain nozzle and pipe two rounds, each measuring 8 inches (20 cm.) across, on baking sheets lined with greased paper or foil. Put the remaining meringue in the bag with a star nozzle and pipe a shell border round the edge of one round. Cook in a very cool oven until dried out. These keep very well in a tin for a few days.

For the filling, stew the blackberries with the sugar until tender and leave to cool. Cook the pears in the juice of the blackberries if using fresh ones, or drain from their juice if using canned. Strain the juice and thicken with the cornflour. Spread half the whipped cream over the surface of the plain round and top with most of the blackberries. Put the other round on top, spread with the rest of the cream and arrange the pears and remaining blackberries on top. Spoon over the cold juice and serve.

Although all the fruit can be cooked in advance, and the juice thickened, do not assemble the pudding more than 1 hour in advance, or it may go soft.
Cooking time several hours
Oven temperature 225°F., 110°C., Gas Mark ¼
Illustrated on page 63

Menu two **Aubergine and tomato casserole**

Imperial/Metric	American
6–8 aubergines, depending on size	6–8 eggplants, depending on size
salt	salt
oil	oil
2 lb./900 g. tomatoes	2 lb. tomatoes
butter	butter
black pepper	black pepper
6 oz./175 g. mild Cheddar cheese, grated	1½ cups grated mild Cheddar cheese
½ pint/3 dl. single cream	1¼ cups coffee cream
2 oz./50 g. breadcrumbs	1 cup bread crumbs

Wash the aubergines and cut into thin slices, sprinkle with salt and leave to drain in a colander for 1 hour. Wipe the aubergines with a paper towel, heat a little oil and lightly fry the slices, then drain on absorbent paper. Peel and slice the tomatoes. Butter a deep ovenproof dish; place a layer of aubergine slices on the bottom, season with black pepper, sprinkle on a little cheese and cream, cover with a layer of tomatoes and continue with these layers until all the vegetables are used. Finish with a layer of aubergines, sprinkle well with cream, cheese and breadcrumbs, dot with butter and cook in a moderately hot oven for about 45 minutes.
Cooking time about 45 minutes
Oven temperature 375°F., 190°C., Gas Mark 5

Salmon and cheese quiche

Imperial/Metric	American
6 oz./175 g. shortcrust pastry	basic pie dough made with 1½ cups flour
1 can salmon	1 can salmon
½ onion, grated or very finely chopped	½ onion, grated or very finely chopped
2 oz./50 g. Cheddar cheese, grated	½ cup grated Cheddar cheese
2 eggs	2 eggs
¼ pint/1½ dl. milk	⅔ cup milk
salt and pepper	salt and pepper
chopped parsley	chopped parsley

Line an 8-inch (20-cm.) flan tin with the pastry and bake blind for 10 minutes. Flake the salmon, removing all the skin and bones. Put the fish on the bottom of the flan. Sprinkle the onion over the top, and the cheese on top of that. Beat the eggs with the milk and season well. Pour on to the flan and sprinkle with chopped parsley. Bake in the centre of a moderately hot oven for about 30 minutes, until well risen and golden brown. Serve either hot or warm.

This is the best way of using a can of salmon we know. It's always a great success with the men of the family.
Cooking time about 40 minutes
Oven temperature 375°F., 190°C., Gas Mark 5

Quiche lorraine

This filling is for an 8-inch (20-cm.) pastry case. Since it's for a party we suggest partially baking the case in the morning and preparing the filling and refrigerating it. Half an hour before you require the quiche, pour the filling into the case and place in a moderately hot oven. The quiche will stay puffed for 10 minutes after cooking if it's kept in a hot oven with the door slightly open, but will fall as it cools.

Imperial/Metric	American
4 oz./100 g. streaky bacon	5 slices bacon
1 8-inch/20-cm. pastry case, baked blind	1 8-inch pie shell, baked blind
3 eggs	3 eggs
¼ pint/1½ dl. single cream	⅔ cup coffee cream
¼ pint/1½ dl. milk	⅔ cup milk
salt	salt
pinch nutmeg	pinch nutmeg
white pepper	white pepper
knob of butter	knob of butter

Remove the rind from the bacon, cut into small pieces and lightly fry, drain. Put the bacon on the bottom of the pastry case. Beat the eggs with the cream and milk and seasonings. Pour into the pastry case and dot with butter. Cook in a moderately hot oven for 30 minutes.
Cooking time 30 minutes
Oven temperature 375°F., 190°C., Gas Mark 5

Variations
Add a little chopped onion, lightly fried, or a little grated cheese.
Kipper and sour cream quiche Blend in the liquidiser until really smooth an 8-oz. (227-g.) packet kipper fillets with ¼ pint (1½ dl., ⅔ cup) sour cream, 1 egg, 2 tablespoons milk, salt and pepper and 1 teaspoon chopped parsley. Pour into the *unbaked* pastry case and cook for 35–40 minutes. Garnish with tomato slices.

Chicken and gammon pie

Imperial/Metric	American
1 3½-lb./1½-kg. chicken, boned (keep the bones)	1 3½-lb. chicken, boned (keep the bones)
1 stalk celery	1 stalk celery
1 carrot	1 carrot
2 onions	2 onions
salt and pepper	salt and pepper
1 8-oz./225-g. gammon rasher	1 ½-lb. piece ham, butt half
hot water pastry	hot water crust
3 oz./75 g. lard	6 tablespoons lard
¼ pint/1½ dl. water	⅔ cup water
12 oz./350 g. plain flour	3 cups all-purpose flour
egg and milk to glaze	egg and milk to glaze

Take all the flesh off the chicken, using a small sharp knife. Put the skin and bones with the giblets in a saucepan and add the celery, carrot, and 1 onion, cut up roughly. Season, cover with water, bring to the boil and simmer to make a good stock. This takes 2–3 hours.

Meanwhile, cut the chicken flesh into ½-inch (1-cm.) pieces and put in a bowl. Trim the rind from the gammon and cut up into ½-inch (1-cm.) pieces also. Add to the chicken with the remaining onion, finely chopped, season and mix well.

To make the pastry, put the lard and water into a small saucepan and heat gently. Put the flour into a mixing bowl, and when the lard has melted bring the water to the boil and pour quickly into the flour, stirring well. When the pastry is cool enough to handle knead together with the fingers until the flour is all mixed in. Add another tablespoon of water if necessary.

Preheat the oven to moderate and line the base of a loose-bottomed 8-inch (20-cm.) cake tin. Cut off a third of the pastry and reserve for the lid. Put the larger piece in the prepared tin and press out with the fingers to line the base and sides evenly. Make sure there are no cracks. Fill the case loosely with the meat mixture and moisten with 1 tablespoon of the stock. Roll out the remaining pastry on a floured board to slightly larger than the tin, damp the edges of the case, lift the lid on and press the edges together, cutting off any extra pastry. Make a decorative edge, roll out the trimmings and cut into leaf shapes. Damp these and fix on top of the pie. Make a hole in the middle. Brush with egg and milk to glaze and put in the preheated oven for 1¼ hours. Lift carefully out of the tin and brush the sides with glaze. Return for 5 minutes. Remove and leave to cool for at least 2 hours.

Reduce the stock until there is about ½ pint (3 dl./1¼ cups) left by boiling rapidly without a lid. Strain and leave to cool. Fill the pie through the hole in the middle with the cool stock when it is just about to set to jelly. Leave the pie to cool for several hours, or overnight, before serving.

Cooking time 1 hour 20 minutes
Oven temperature 350°F., 180°C., Gas Mark 4

Mixed green salad

Wash 3 large lettuces and drain well, then dry in a tea towel. Tear up the leaves and put into a salad bowl. Add a bunch of watercress, washed, in pieces and a chopped or finely sliced green pepper. Just before serving toss with ¼ pint (1½ dl., ⅔ cup) French dressing.

Liquidiser mayonnaise

Imperial/Metric	American
1 egg	1 egg
½ teaspoon salt	½ teaspoon salt
¼ teaspoon mustard	¼ teaspoon mustard
¼ teaspoon castor sugar	¼ teaspoon granulated sugar
2 tablespoons vinegar	3 tablespoons vinegar
½ pint/3 dl. oil	1¼ cups oil

Place all the ingredients except the oil in the liquidiser and blend until well mixed. Remove the small cap in the lid of the jar, or failing that make a foil cover with a hole in the middle. Switch on the blender and very slowly pour in the oil until the mayonnaise is thick and creamy. Keep in the fridge.

Celery, apple and peanut salad

This is particularly good with cold chicken and turkey.

Imperial/Metric	American
6 stalks celery	6 stalks celery
3 crisp eating apples	3 crisp eating apples
juice of ½ lemon	juice of ½ lemon
4 tablespoons French dressing	⅓ cup French dressing
3–4 oz./75–100 g. salted peanuts	½–⅔ cup salted peanuts
¼ onion, finely chopped	¼ onion, finely chopped

Slice the celery and put into a bowl. Coarsely grate the peeled apples and add to the celery. Add the lemon juice and dressing and mix well. Stir in the peanuts and the onion and cover until ready to serve.

Tomatoes with onion rings and chives

Imperial/Metric	American
12 tomatoes, sliced	12 tomatoes, sliced
2 small onions	2 small onions
¼ pint/1½ dl. French dressing	⅔ cup French dressing
1 tablespoon chopped chives	1 tablespoon chopped chives

Put the sliced tomatoes in a dish and cover with the onions cut into paper-thin rings. Pour over the French dressing and sprinkle the chives over the top.

Spanish potato salad

Imperial/Metric	American
5 lb./2¼ kg. potatoes	5 lb. potatoes
1 medium-sized onion	1 medium-sized onion
4 hard-boiled eggs	4 hard-cooked eggs
gherkins	dill pickles
mayonnaise	mayonnaise
salt and pepper	salt and pepper
lettuce leaves	lettuce leaves
1 small can pimentos	1 small can pimientos
green olives	green olives

Peel the potatoes and cook in plenty of salted boiling water. When well cooked, drain thoroughly and cut into small dice. Put the cool potatoes in a large bowl. Peel and finely chop the onion, chop two of the eggs, and chop 6–8 gherkins; add all these to the potatoes, stir in plenty of mayonnaise, salt and pepper to taste and mix until well blended. Pile the potato salad on an oblong dish or plate and shape into a large oval; flatten the top. Coat with a little more mayonnaise. Decorate with a few lettuce leaves around the dish, and decorate the sides and top of the potatoes with the remaining eggs sliced thinly, strips of pimento, sliced olives, fans cut from the gherkins and anything else suitable.

Chocolate gâteau

Imperial/Metric	American
cake base	cake base
4 oz./100 g. castor sugar	½ cup granulated sugar
4 eggs	4 eggs
4 oz./100 g. plain chocolate	⅔ cup semi-sweet chocolate pieces
4 oz./100 g. ground almonds	1 cup ground almonds

topping	topping
½ pint/3 dl. double cream	1¼ cups heavy cream
2–3 tablespoons brandy	3–4 tablespoons brandy
4 oz./100 g. plain chocolate	⅔ cup semi-sweet chocolate pieces
½ oz. butter	1 tablespoon butter
2 tablespoons strong black coffee	3 tablespoons strong black coffee

Put the sugar and eggs in a large basin and beat together for 10–15 minutes with an electric beater. Meanwhile melt the chocolate and allow to cool slightly. Add the almonds and chocolate to the egg mixture and fold in gently with a metal spoon. Pour into a well-greased round 10-inch (25-cm.) cake tin with a removable base and bake in a moderate oven for 30–40 minutes. Allow to cool in the tin, then turn out on to a serving dish. Cover and leave overnight if possible.

To make the topping, beat the cream and brandy together until thick and spread over the cake to cover it completely. Melt the chocolate, butter and coffee together and when cool dribble over the cream.

Cooking time 30–40 minutes

Oven temperature 325°F., 160°C., Gas Mark 3

Strawberry and raspberry mousse

Imperial/Metric	American
1 15-oz./425-g. can strawberries	1 15-oz. can strawberries
1 raspberry jelly	1 package raspberry-flavored gelatin
3 eggs, separated	3 eggs, separated
1 oz./25 g. sugar	2 tablespoons sugar
¼ pint/1½ dl. double cream	⅔ cup whipping cream

Put the strawberries in the blender and liquidise until smooth. Make the purée up to ¾ pint (4 dl., 1¼ cups) with water, pour into a saucepan and bring to the boil. Take off the heat and add the raspberry jelly. Stir until melted and cool. Beat the egg yolks and sugar in a large bowl until thick and light, then gradually whisk in the liquid jelly. Set aside until cool, whisking from time to time until just beginning to thicken. Whisk the egg whites until stiff and the cream until thick but not stiff, and fold both into the fruit mixture. Blend well and pour into a glass serving dish. Chill well and decorate the top with whipped cream.

Useful facts and figures

NOTE ON METRICATION

In this book quantities have been given in both metric and Imperial measures. Exact conversion from Imperial to metric measures does not usually give very convenient working quantities and so for greater convenience we have rounded off metric measures into units of 25 grammes. The table below shows recommended equivalents.

Ounces/fluid ounces	Approx. g. and ml. to nearest whole figure	Recommended conversion to nearest unit of 25
1	28	25
2	57	50
3	85	75
4	113	100
5 ($\frac{1}{4}$ pint)	142	150
6	170	175
7	198	200
8 ($\frac{1}{4}$ lb.)	226	225
9	255	250
10 ($\frac{1}{2}$ pint)	283	275
11	311	300
12	340	350
13	368	375
14	396	400
15 ($\frac{3}{4}$ pint)	428	425
16 (1 lb.)	456	450
17	484	475
18	512	500
19	541	550
20 (1 pint)	569	575

Note When converting quantities over 20 oz. first add the appropriate figures in the centre column, *then* adjust to the nearest unit of 25. As a general guide, 1 kg. (1000 g.) equals 2·2 lb. or about 2 lb. 3 oz.; 1 litre (1000 ml.) equals 1·76 pints or almost exactly 1$\frac{3}{4}$ pints.

Liquid measures

The millilitre is a very small unit of measurement and we felt that to use decilitres (units of 100 ml.) would be less cumbersome. In most cases it is perfectly satisfactory to round off the exact millilitre conversion to the nearest decilitre, except for $\frac{1}{4}$ pint; thus $\frac{1}{4}$ pint (142 ml.) is 1$\frac{1}{2}$ dl., $\frac{1}{2}$ pint (283 ml.) is 3 dl., $\frac{3}{4}$ pint (428 ml.) is 4 dl., and 1 pint (569 ml.) is 6 dl. For quantities over 1 pint we have used litres and fractions of a litre.

Can sizes

Because at present cans are marked with the exact (usually to the nearest whole number) metric equivalent of the Imperial weight of the contents, we have followed this practice when giving can sizes. Thus the equivalent of a 14-oz. can of tomatoes would be a 396-g. can.

OVEN TEMPERATURES

The chart below gives recommended Celsius (Centigrade) equivalents.

Description	Fahrenheit	Celsius	Gas Mark
Very cool	225	110	$\frac{1}{4}$
	250	120	$\frac{1}{2}$
Cool	275	140	1
	300	150	2
Moderate	325	160	3
	350	180	4
Moderately hot	375	190	5
	400	200	6
Hot	425	220	7
	450	230	8
Very hot	475	240	9

NOTES FOR AMERICAN USERS

In the recipes in this book quantities are given in American standard cup and spoon measures as well as Imperial and metric measures. The list below gives some American equivalents or substitutes for terms or ingredients.

BRITISH	AMERICAN
basin	bowl
baking tin	baking pan
cochineal	red food coloring
cocktail stick	wooden toothpick
deep cake tin	springform pan
fillet	tenderloin
frying pan	skillet
greaseproof paper	wax paper
grill	broil/broiler
kitchen paper	paper towels
liquidiser	blender
muslin	cheesecloth
mince	grind/ground beef
piping bag	pastry bag
pie dish	baking dish
sandwich tin	layer cake pan
stoned	pitted
swiss roll tin	jelly roll pan
sweet	candy
vanilla pod	vanilla bean
whisk	beat/whip

NOTES FOR AUSTRALIAN USERS

Quantities in the recipes in this book are given in metric, Imperial and American measures. The old Australian standard measuring cup is the same as the American standard 8-fluid ounce cup; the new Australian cup is bigger and holds 250 ml. Note also that the Australian standard tablespoon holds 20 ml. and is therefore bigger than either the American (14·2 ml.) or the Imperial (17·7 ml.). The table below gives a comparison.

AMERICAN	BRITISH	AUSTRALIAN
1 teaspoon	1 teaspoon	1 teaspoon
1 tablespoon	1 tablespoon	1 tablespoon
3 tablespoons	2 tablespoons	2 tablespoons
4 tablespoons	3$\frac{1}{2}$ tablespoons	3 tablespoons
5 tablespoons	4 tablespoons	3$\frac{1}{2}$ tablespoons